Managing Consultants

A PRACTICAL GUIDE FOR BUSY
PUBLIC SECTOR MANAGERS

Managing Consultants

A PRACTICAL GUIDE FOR BUSY
PUBLIC SECTOR MANAGERS

LEO DOBES

Australian
National
University

PRESS

ANU PRESS

the Australia and New Zealand
School of Government

Published by ANU Press
The Australian National University
Acton ACT 2601, Australia
Email: anupress@anu.edu.au
This title is also available online at press.anu.edu.au

National Library of Australia Cataloguing-in-Publication entry

Creator:	Dobes, Leo, author.
Title:	Managing consultants : a practical guide for busy public sector managers / Leo Dobes.
Edition:	Second edition.
ISBN:	9781760460464 (paperback) 9781760460471 (ebook)
Series:	Australia and New Zealand School of Government monograph.
Subjects:	Government consultants--Australia. Contracting out--Australia--Management.
Dewey Number:	352.3730994

Cover design and layout by ANU Press. Cover photograph adapted from: 'Well-dressed executives in movement' by pressfoto/freepik.

Contents

About the author

After gaining his BA (Hons) and MA in Economics at the University of Melbourne, Leo Dobes completed a DPhil in East European Economics at the University of Oxford in 1980. His public service career of almost 30 years, much of it at the senior executive level, included the Australian diplomatic service, intelligence analysis in the Office of National Assessments, and provision of policy advice in the Commonwealth departments of Defence, The Treasury, Communications (where he played a key role in developing and implementing the reform of the telecommunications sector in 1990–91) and Transport, including the Bureau of Transport Economics. Dr Dobes also spent a year on secondment at Ernst & Young, prior to market testing and outsourcing various aspects of corporate services in the Department of Transport and Regional Services.

Following his retirement from the Australian Public Service in 2006, Dr Dobes has been at the Crawford School of Public Policy at The Australian National University in Canberra, where he is an honorary Associate Professor. He teaches a regular Masters-level course on Cost–Benefit Analysis, and his research interests currently include the treatment of uncertainty in Cost–Benefit Analysis, adaptation to climate change and the non-unification of the railway gauges following Federation in the early twentieth century.

Foreword

Foreword to the 2006 edition

In this monograph, Leo Dobes has produced something unusual in the annals of the literature on government and public administration: namely, a practical, user-friendly guide to the benefits, perils and pitfalls of managing outside consultants.

He writes from years of experience in managing consultants in government. Dr Dobes has not only produced a guide to best practice, but has also included advice on what not to do, and how to rectify shortcomings in the process of using consultants effectively.

The use of consultants by public sector organisations has grown immensely over the past 10 to 15 years. In many respects, public sector organisations are now dependent upon external consultants for services ranging from facilities management to internal auditing and human resource management to the provision of policy advice (and much in between).

In part, the shift towards dependency has been driven by the implementation of market testing and outsourcing regimes. In part, too, it marks a recognition of gaps in the skill sets existing within the traditional public service and public sector operations that increasingly emulate commercial business practices. Critically, it has been argued in some quarters that the present reliance on external providers of consultancy services has led to a commensurate loss of corporate knowledge about public sector organisations' operations.

In this publication, Dr Dobes warns that despite considerable investment in skills development, managers in public sector organisations may still exhibit significant deficiencies in contract and relationship management skills and knowledge. This monograph is written to redress these deficiencies.

Foreword to the 2016 edition

Much has changed during the decade since the first edition of this monograph. The entire resource management framework of the Australian Government has been revamped, and procurement principles and policy with it.

The large number of 'hits' and downloads of the monograph made it imperative to produce an up-to-date version that would assist government officials to undertake procurement activity with a degree of confidence because of a wider understanding than that available from legislative provisions alone.

Professor John Wanna
Sir John Bunting Chair of Public Administration, Director of Research, Australia and New Zealand School of Government

Preface

Preface to the 2006 edition

Although this publication was commissioned by the Australia and New Zealand School of Government (ANZSOG), the first draft was completed in early 2000, just after I completed a one-year secondment in the Canberra office of Ernst & Young (E&Y).

It became clear during my secondment to E&Y that there was no practical guide on the engagement of consultants available to Australian Public Service managers. It was also clear that many public servants in Canberra simply did not understand how consultants work, and therefore did not obtain as much value for money as they might have otherwise.

The main perspective was necessarily that of an Australian Government public servant. But because most ANZSOG participating governments subscribe to similar principles and policies in their procurement policies, the material differences between them are not substantial. Nevertheless, any significant differences in approach have been noted as far as practicable throughout.

To ensure the capture of as much practical experience as possible, I interviewed 31 practitioners from Australian Government agencies (including the then OASITO, AusAID, ANAO, FACS, DEWR, DOTARS, Defence, and Finance), medium and large consulting firms (ACIL, KPMG, Ernst & Young, SMS Consulting, the then Arthur Anderson, the Centre for International Economics, PriceWaterhouse, and Eltom Consulting), relevant secretariats of parliamentary committees, and the Institution of Engineers Australia. Many of those who were generous enough to share their insights, or to comment on early drafts, have since moved on, and some did not wish to be identified. I am nevertheless grateful to all of them.

The publication has also benefited from the 18 months during which I led a team that market-tested a range of corporate services within the Department of Transport and Regional Services. However, the views expressed here are entirely my own.

Finally, my thanks to Professor Allan Fels for facilitating my participation in ANZSOG teaching activities, to Professor Glenn Withers for encouraging finalisation of the publication, and to Professor John Wanna for some very useful pre-publication comments that helped improve both style and content.

Preface to the 2016 edition

Much has changed in the decade since publication of the first edition in 2006. In particular, the *Financial Management and Accountability Act (FMA) Act 1997* has been replaced by the *Public Governance, Performance and Accountability Act 2013* and its associated instruments. Given the continuing large number of downloads of the 2006 edition, it was considered desirable to update references to the legislative requirements that now govern the Australian Government's procurement principles.

My wife Alice provided invaluable support by identifying and locating relevant documents. I am very much in her debt for this, and much else besides.

Leo Dobes

Abbreviations

AAI	Accountable Authority Instruction
ABN	Australian Business Number
ATM	approach to market
CCE	Corporate Commonwealth Entity
CCS	Commonwealth Contracting Suite
CPG	Commonwealth Procurement Guidelines
CPR	Commonwealth Procurement Rules
EOI	Expression of Interest
GST	Goods and Services Tax
NCCE	Non-Corporate Commonwealth Entity
PGPA Act	*Public Governance, Performance and Accountability Act 2013*
PGPAR	*Public Governance, Performance and Accountability Rule 2014*
RMG	Resource Management Guide
RFT	Request for Tender
SES	Senior Executive Service
SME	Small and Medium Enterprise

Using this guide

The chapters in this monograph are generally divided into four sections as set out below and illustrated in Figure 1 (overleaf):

Some basics: a general guide for those who do not regularly let contracts.

Australian Government requirements: a summary of compulsory provisions, as well as policy and best practice 'should do' items.

Risk management: generic information to save reinventing the wheel.

Tips and traps: a compendium of experiences in the public and private sectors.

Project stages

Some basics

- Provides summary of essentials
- Matched to stages of a project
- Balances basic principles with modern practice

Establish need

Tender documents

Australian Government requirements

- Mandatory requirements and policy guidelines
- PGPA Act and associated instruments, including the Commonwealth Procurement Rules

Fees & expenses

Choose consultant

Risk management

Risk	Consequence	Mitigation
• Ignorance	• Problems	• Read this book
• Out-of-date information	• Problems	• Read this book
• Process focus	• Problems	• Read this book

Agree contract

Contract management

Closure

Tips and traps

- First hand practitioner knowledge
- Private sector consultants
- Public service managers

Evaulation

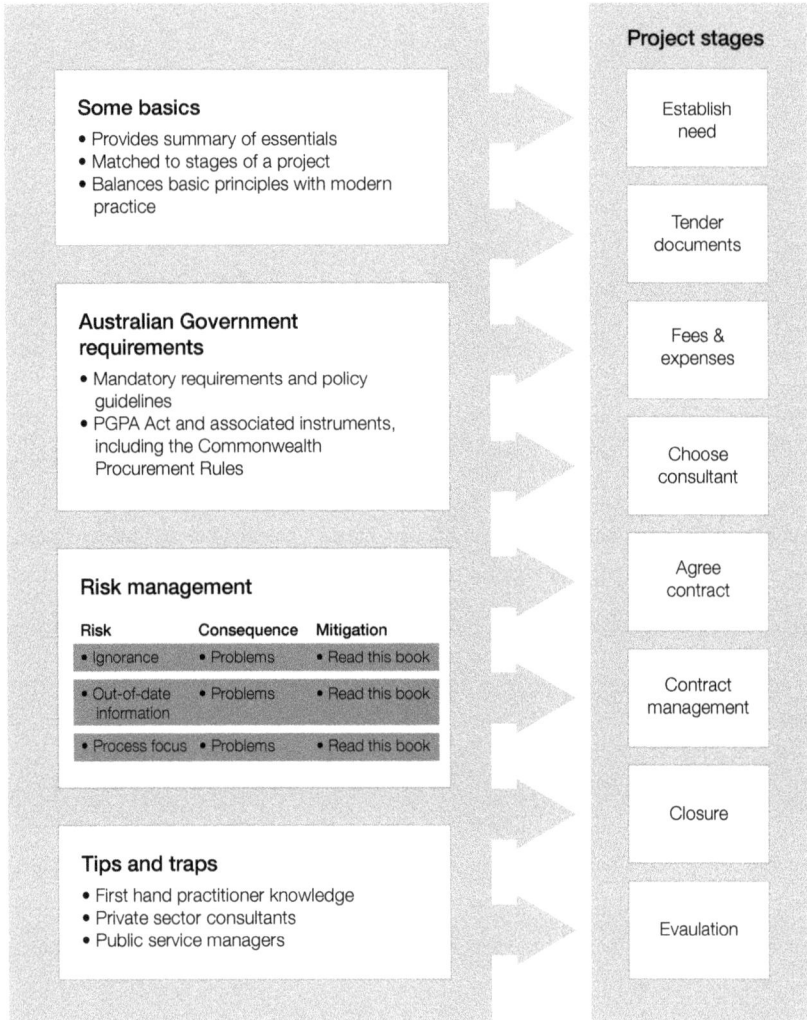

Figure 1. How to use this guide

1

Understanding how consultants work

Some basics

Consultants are people with skills or expertise who provide advice that assists managers to make decisions. Contracts with consultants generally specify the purpose of the task, but not details or the manner in which it is to be performed. In general, one would expect a consultant to work independently, use their own equipment, be engaged in developing a new concept or approach or process by applying their own judgement or specific expertise, and be paid according to milestones achieved. Contractors, on the other hand, are usually engaged and paid by the hour to deliver defined goods or services or prescribed tasks as a result of decisions already taken by an agency. In some cases, a contractor may technically be considered to be an employee of an agency, even if engaged under a specific contract.

It may be difficult to distinguish between contractors, consultants and employees. The distinction can be important because Non-Corporate Commonwealth Entities are required to report the use of consultancy services on AusTender (see Chapter 3). Depending on the terms of engagement, there may also be inconspicuous legal implications concerning fees, taxation, superannuation or liability for workers' compensation. Before initiating a procurement process, it is worth checking the prospective status with a relevant Human Resources or legal area, as well as the Accountable Authority Instructions (previously called Chief Executive Instructions) for the entity.

Understanding consultants and their ways

Unlike public service employees, consultants are engaged on a temporary basis to carry out specific projects. Establishing a collaborative relationship with consultants, therefore, requires some understanding of their working methods and environment.

Public service characterisations of consultants sometimes portray them as grossly overpaid, willing to take on any job, even at short notice, and being happy to work through the night or weekend to complete it, invariably late with reports, requiring a lot of teaching to be able to do the job, and seldom capable of producing the quality of work that could have been achieved in-house by a public servant.

Consultants are more circumspect about their public servant clients. Pressed, they often express concern about clients who have not entirely thought through their requirements for a job, or who leave things until the last minute and then expect a high quality proposal or solution to a problem overnight. However, most are also anxious that their reports not be left to simply gather dust on a bookshelf. Like public servants, they have a professional interest and pride in seeing their advice being implemented.

There is often some element of truth to stereotypes and popular images, even if they are exaggerated. But a productive relationship needs to be based on knowledge. If you are unsure about some aspect of a consultant's behaviour, then ask them. Consultants are human, despite some of the myths.

A number of points may also help clarify some of the more frequent misconceptions:

- The atmosphere in a consulting firm is usually more intense than in a public service office. Consultants' days are rather focused; they must fill in time sheets that distinguish between chargeable and non-chargeable use of their time. Meetings tend to be shorter and involve fewer people than those in the public service. The 'time is money' philosophy applies. On the other hand, a good consultancy office also has a supportive culture that encourages the sharing of information and celebration of employees' successes.

- Don't be too surprised by consultants' apparent rates of remuneration. Their firm usually charges clients some multiple of their salary to cover administrative overheads, or to allow for expertise drawn upon elsewhere in the firm. Some independent consultants may earn seemingly large daily amounts, but, unlike wage and salary earners, they do not always have a steady income.

- Because of the need to compensate for lack of steady income, most consultants need to work on at least three or four projects at any one time. Only in the case of very large projects are they dedicated solely to one client, although they may still be expected to help colleagues in other areas. While you should always expect that a consultant will be responsive to your needs, you need to recognise that their time is not devoted entirely to you unless they are contractually obliged that it be so. But that should not matter, provided that the work is done on time and to an acceptable standard.

- Because of the uncertainty of obtaining work, consultants will often put forward bids for more work than they can actually handle. If too many bids are successful, 'bunching' of workloads can cause problems for them and their clients. As a result, a consultant may sometimes seek to delay work or to redefine the scope of the project.

- Consultants often have families. And they like to catch up on some relaxation over the weekend, even if (like many public servants) they also devote some of their leisure time to work.

- Experienced consultants may choose not to bid for work. Clients with reputations for bad project management (particularly lack of clarity in objectives) tend to be avoided. Even existing clients who offer additional work on a 'messy' project may find that they are politely refused, often with the excuse that the consultant is already committed elsewhere. However, it is more likely that a consultant will not put forward a bid because:
  - the client is not a major user of consultancy services and repeat work is unlikely;
  - the return calculated within the consulting firm's internal budgetary processes is too low; or,
  - the potential client is not among the consulting firm's strategic targets.

- For example, the firm may be targeting clients who are likely to need the existing skills of its consultants for some time and servicing a new client would require investment of time to develop new capabilities.

- An occasional complaint is that it is often necessary to teach a consultant about an issue. True, but it also masks a misunderstanding about the role of a consultant. A consultant is hired for specific skills such as being able to manage organisational change, or ability to analyse data. Unless the consultant is used regularly by the client, he or she will initially need to rely on the client for information on the agency's business processes, legislation, or political considerations. If used in complementary ways, the respective skills of the consultant and the client will produce a better output.

- You may have noticed that some of your consultant contacts spend a lot of time in coffee shops. This is not an indication of attempts to overdose on caffeine, nor does it indicate an easy life. On the contrary, the pressure of 'billable' time may mean that it is more efficient to work in a coffee shop in between appointments with clients, rather than going back and forth to an office (if indeed the consultant has an office). And besides, one meets more business contacts in a coffee shop; something that has been well known for several hundred years.

- Consultancy firms tend to have flatter management structures than those in the public service. (The title on a business card may not be a good indicator of relative position in the firm because it may simply be used to impress clients.) Most large firms have structures something similar to that set out in Figure 2, although titles can differ between companies:

PARTNER

(about the pay-equivalent of an SES
officer, but may be paid more)

PRINCIPAL

(similar level to a partner, but
without equity in the firm)

DIRECTOR/EXECUTIVE CONSULTANT

SENIOR MANAGER/SENIOR CONSULTANT

CONSULTANT

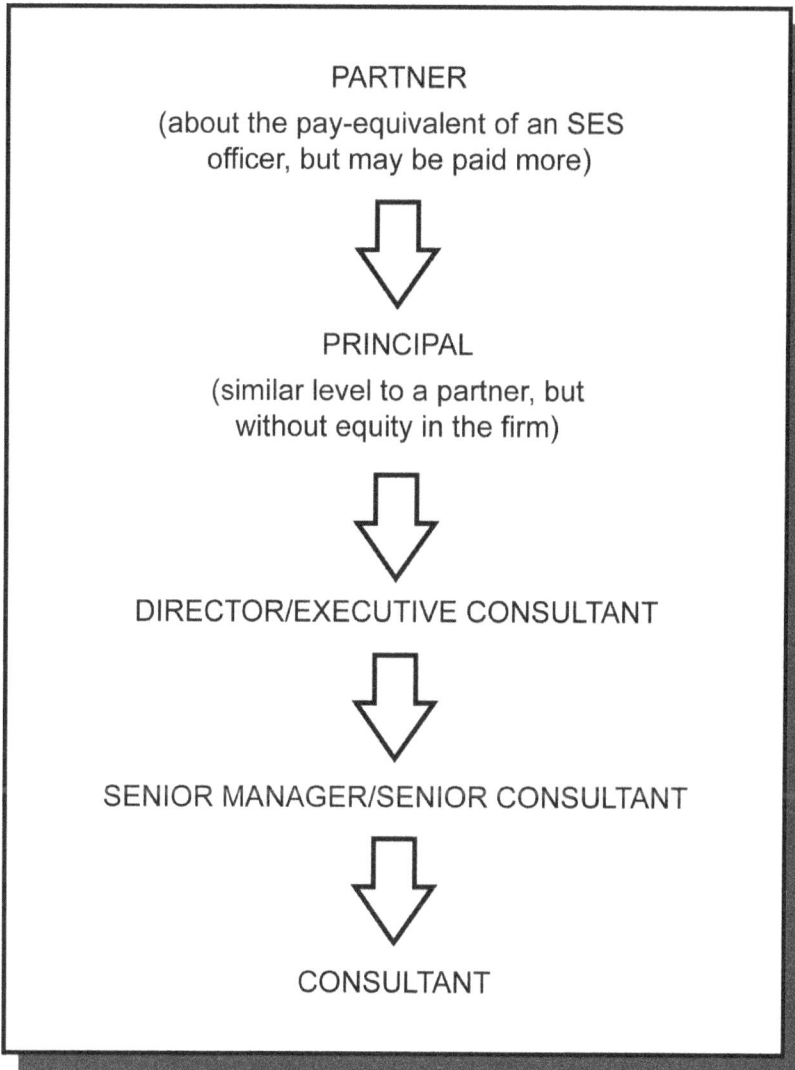

Figure 2. Illustrative hierarchy of a consulting firm

Exhibit 1.1. A day in the life of Mike, a senior consultant at a large firm

8:00 am   Mike logs into the firm's network remotely at home, checking for emails received since last night. He responds to the urgent ones, as well as replying to a few from clients and colleagues. The main message is from a Department A client who wants to meet at 1.30 pm, prior to a steering committee meeting. The same message has been left on his mobile phone. Mike emails a confirmation.

8:30 am   Like many people, Mike delivers the kids to school. Having dropped them off, he checks for messages on his (hands-free) mobile phone as he drives to work.

His first appointment for the day is at a coffee shop near a client's office: a fairly central site where he and some of his colleagues tend to meet. He especially needs to catch up with Jane, who has been working at a client's premises for a couple of weeks.

Following some quick pleasantries, Mike and his colleagues agree on responsibilities for putting together a major project proposal, which is due in five days (the tender documents were only obtained yesterday). Their biggest problem is in working out exactly what the client wants done. Katrina volunteers to call the contact officer to seek clarification.

9:30 am   Mike drives to his office, checks for phone messages (he has only one) and his emails. He makes a call to a colleague to chase up a performance report he needs for a staff member's performance review and another to confirm attendance and arrangements for a presentation he will be giving in Melbourne on Thursday.

One of his emails is a bit worrying because he can't meet a request from client B for a meeting on Thursday. He calls to discuss this with the client and explains that he has another appointment (the presentation in Melbourne), but should be able to get back for an afternoon meeting. But client B is still unhappy.

Seeking out a colleague, Mike blows off a bit of steam, but the two agree that it is best to keep client B happy: there is good potential for follow-on work. They agree that if an afternoon meeting is not possible, Leonie will go instead of Mike.

Mike finds a 'quiet room'. His firm switched recently to an open plan, 'hot desking' layout and there are no workstations available at the moment. He begins editing a report due by the end of the day. He switches off his mobile and asks the personal assistant, whose services he shares with 12 colleagues, to tell callers that he is in a meeting and will call back soon.

Sandwiches with David, one of the firm's partners, in the ground-floor shop, partly to review progress on a number of jobs, partly to discuss forthcoming staff performance reviews and partly to just stay in touch. Mike is interrupted during lunch by a call on his mobile. As is often the case, David fields at least two calls in the same time.

1:00 pm   After responding to several new emails, Mike heads off to a steering committee meeting for one of the two projects he is currently working on at Department A. He starts to mentally prioritise next week's commitments when David calls. Mike is asked to drop in on another client to review a colleague's report with which the client is not happy.

1:30 pm   A brief 'heads up' meeting with the Department A project director to discuss tactics before the steering committee meeting. The project is already falling behind schedule. If it is to be finished on time, they need to convince one of the more influential committee members to stop insisting on more work in an interesting, but essentially peripheral area. The extra work is not specified in the terms of reference for the project or in the contract.

2:00 pm   The adrenaline flows as Mike presents a detailed progress report. He manages to have the additional work deferred until after the conclusion of this project, but timelines can't move: the draft report is due next Friday.

3:15 pm   Mike and the project director hold a 'wash-up meeting' after the steering committee meeting and discuss a first draft of the report. Mike seeks the project director's feedback on the meeting as well as input on the suggested format, content and structure of the report.

            There is some pressure now from the project director to undertake at least some of the extra work before Friday to keep the steering committee happy. However, he understands that this is additional work and offers to draw up a variation to the contract for an extra three days work at a slightly higher fee in acknowledgment of the difficulties involved.

4:00 pm   On his way back to the office, Mike assesses his commitments and begins a series of calls to try to push out other work by a few days to give himself the time he needs. Other clients are reluctant to change their expectations, but he does manage to gain some additional time into next week.

4:30 pm   Checking his email and phone messages again in the office, Mike resolves a diary clash. He also adds the finishing touches to a draft report due this afternoon and emails it to client C with a covering note. He then calls the client to let him know that it has been sent and to arrange a meeting for next week to discuss it.

5:15 pm   After catching up briefly with some of his colleagues who have also just returned, Mike updates his timesheet for the last few days (this is supposed to be done daily but he has been too busy). The end of the month is approaching, so he also starts going through the timesheet printouts to prepare client invoices for the month. He doesn't want the managing partner on his back again.

            Mike realises that today was not a good billable day. His 'utilisation' rate was only about 60 per cent, well below his budget target. Although yesterday was a high utilisation day, any surplus has been brought down by today's performance.

6.10 pm   Just before going home, Mike receives a call from Peter, a consultant with another firm. Peter has been thinking of going into consulting on his own and asks Mike, who used to run his own consulting business a few years ago, for advice.

Peter worries about whether he could support his current level of income, how he would get work and whether he has a good enough network of contacts to support himself as a single consultant on his own. He has heard of a colleague who struggled for the first 12 months because some clients took so long to pay their bills.

6:40 pm   Driving home, Mike makes a mental note to check his travel arrangements for Thursday.

9.15 pm   With dinner over, and the kids in bed, Mike settles in with his laptop for an hour's work on the draft report, and to check and send some emails. He also needs to review the reports emailed to him for the performance review that he has to conduct first thing tomorrow morning.

2

Establishing the need
for a consultant

Some basics

Busy managers often have little patience with advice that suggests careful planning and consideration at the outset. Their impatience is understandable. Experience, however, has shown that much time and effort can be saved over the course of a project if a few extra hours are invested at the beginning. Defining the problem, considering alternatives and drafting a clear statement of requirement are key factors in minimising potential problems later on.

Recourse to external consultancy services should, in normal circumstances, occur only after carrying out, and documenting for file, a business case which addresses the following:

- a clear exposition of the problem or issue being solved: both consultants and experienced public sector users of consultancy services stress that clarity of purpose is the key factor in a successful tender process;

- relevance to government policy or programs, including coordination with other entities;

- scope and quality of outputs required;

- the timeframe for completion;

- whether the proposal was included in the entity's Annual Procurement Plan;
- likely GST-inclusive cost (fees *and* expenses) and availability of funding, including a contingency allowance, compared to benefits gained;
- degree of any required skill transfer to the entity;
- security considerations, including access to classified information;
- the alternative of carrying out the work in-house; and,
- how value for money will be achieved on the basis of clauses 4.1 to 4.15 of the Commonwealth Procurement Rules (CPRs).

Whether an agency should engage external consultants will often depend on factors such as the following:

- a temporary lack of in-house people resources;
- the need for specialised skills or experience;
- provision of independent advice, either to the entity itself, or to enhance public credibility;
- diagnostic management advice to the entity, including facilitation or management of change;
- a need for advice on how best to meet a new government requirement; and,
- assistance with a review of an agency's service delivery as part of a Performance Improvement Cycle approach.

If unsure of your justification for proceeding with a consultancy, it is worth testing your reasoning with your entity's procurement adviser or the Department of Finance.

Although the justification for hiring external consultancy services will differ according to individual circumstances, the golden rule is that the engagement should provide value for money. The concept of 'value for money' is presented in Chapter 4.

Australian Government requirements

The *Public Governance, Performance and Accountability Act 2013* (PGPA Act) specifies that a Commonwealth entity must be governed in a way that promotes the proper use and management of public resources.

Chapter 2 of the PGPA Act places the onus for promoting the 'proper use and management of public resources' on the accountable authority (that is, the head or Chief Executive, or board) of each Commonwealth entity (e.g. a department or a government corporation). Under the PGPA Act, the accountable authority 'must govern the entity … in a way that is not inconsistent with the policies of the Australian Government', and may issue entity-specific 'Accountable Authority Instructions' (called the Chief Executive's Instructions under previous legislation) to this end to officials of their entity. For their part, officials are required under the PGPA Act to perform their functions 'honestly, in good faith and for a proper purpose'.

In the past, agencies had some latitude in the conduct of procurement processes because the government emphasised achievement of outcomes, rather than the observance of detailed procedures. In January 2005, however, the new Commonwealth Procurement Guidelines (CPGs) introduced a more directive approach. For example, it became virtually mandatory (with some exceptions) to begin with an open tender process in the case of procurements above specified monetary levels; the previous option of moving immediately to a select tender was no longer available.

The CPRs that replaced the CPGs in 2014 appear to have tightened procurement processes further. For example, an official who took action that was inconsistent with the CPGs was able to redress the inconsistency to some extent by making 'a written record of his or her reasons for doing so' (Financial Management Act Regulation 8(2)). The new CPRs do not afford a similar circumvention. On the contrary, it is the 'accountable authority' (the Secretary of the Department in the case of a Commonwealth entity) who must report all known instances of non-compliance in their annual Compliance Report to the minister (Resource Management Guide (RMG) no. 208).

Because it is the primary legislation covering resource management, the PGPA Act sets out the key principles and requirements for a coherent administrative system that emphasises planning, performance and reporting. It is supported by rules and other legislative instruments that provide greater detail about requirements and procedures. The CPRs are one of these legislative instruments.

Commonwealth Procurement Rules

Issued by the Minister for Finance under the PGPA Act, the CPRs came into effect on 1 July 2014. They apply to Non-Corporate Commonwealth Entities (NCCEs) and to the 20 Corporate Commonwealth Entities (CCEs) listed in section 30 of the *Public Governance, Performance and Accountability Rule 2014* (PGPAR). (These two sets of entities are referred to collectively in clause 2.2 of the CPRs as 'relevant entities'.) The CPRs and associated materials are available on the Department of Finance website: www.finance.gov.au/procurement.

The fundamental objective of procurement by entities subject to the PGPA Act is to achieve value for money by delivering the government's programs efficiently, effectively and ethically. Both financial and non-financial costs and benefits need to be considered in any procurement activity.

The CPRs contain two divisions. Division 1 sets out rules for all procurements that are mandatory for all 'relevant entities'. However, NCCEs listed in section 30 of the PGPAR are further subject to 'additional rules' listed in Division 2 of the CPRs where the procurement exceeds a specified total monetary amount ('procurement threshold') and the entity is not otherwise exempted under Appendix A of the CPRs. Both divisions contain mandatory and advisory (best practice) provisions.

Most of the content of the CPRs is reflected throughout this guide. But officials considering the engagement of consultants should always consult the CPRs and their Accountable Authority Instructions directly, as well as any additional web-based guidance issued by the Department of Finance such as the RMG series. The Procurement Policy Branch of the Department of Finance may be another potential source of advice.

Accountable Authority Instructions

Accountable authorities are enabled by the PGPA Act to give instructions regarding finance law to officials in their entities using Accountable Authority Instructions (AAIs) (called the Chief Executive's Instructions in previous legislation). AAIs may cover a large range of matters that involve management of public resources, including procurement.

The Department of Finance (2015) has published model AAIs in RMG no. 206, but relevant entities may differ in their approach to procuring goods and services. A first step in considering the use of a consultant should therefore be to consult the AAIs for the entity concerned. In cases where an official of one Commonwealth entity performs a task for one or more other Commonwealth entities, it will be prudent to first determine which entity's AAIs will apply.

Coordinated and cooperative procurement

Relevant entities need not necessarily take procurement action alone.

It is possible to collaborate with another relevant entity in making a joint approach to market, or even to piggy-back on an existing contract of another relevant entity (CPR clause 4.9). However, it is possible to join an existing contract only if the contract and the request documentation on which it is based have specified the possibility of utilisation by other relevant entities, and the goods and services are comparable to those sought (CPR clause 4.12). In any case, the core principle of achieving value for money must be satisfied.

Where whole-of-government arrangements for procuring goods and services already exist, such arrangements are referred to as 'coordinated procurement'. NCCEs are required to make use of them, rather than approaching the market independently (CPR clauses 4.9 and 4.10). CCEs may also opt-in to coordinated procurement arrangements. A list of existing arrangements that are suitable for coordinated procurement is published online by the Department of Finance www.finance.gov.au/procurement/wog-procurement.

Approval of spending proposals

The accountable authority is responsible under the PGPA Act for promoting the proper use of 'relevant money'; that is, its 'efficient, effective, economical and ethical' use. Where the authority is delegated to an official, the official is required under the PGPA Act to act with care and diligence, and for a proper purpose.

The terms 'efficient, effective, economical and ethical' are not defined in the PGPA Act. Clauses 6.1 to 6.5 of the CPRs provide the following guidance, and point out that, for NCCEs, the collective term 'would also include being not inconsistent with the policies of the Commonwealth':

- Efficient relates to the achievement of the maximum value for the resources used. In procurement, it includes the selection of a procurement method that is the most appropriate for the procurement activity, given the scale, scope and risk of the procurement.
- Effective relates to the extent to which intended outcomes or results are achieved. It concerns the immediate characteristics, especially price, quality and quantity, and the degree to which these contribute to specified outcomes.
- Economical relates to minimising cost. It emphasises the requirement to avoid waste and sharpens the focus on the level of resources that the Commonwealth applies to achieve outcomes.
- Ethical relates to honesty, integrity, probity, diligence, fairness and consistency. Ethical behaviour identifies and manages conflicts of interests, and does not make improper use of an individual's position.

RMG no. 400, issued by the Department of Finance in 2014, includes a more general set of principles of relevance to the broader issue of resource management, rather than just a procurement context. For example, the term economical is stated to emphasise 'the requirement to avoid waste'.

Australian Government public servants are also bound by the Australian Public Service (APS) Values and Code of Conduct under sections 10 and 13 of the *Public Service Act 1999*. Relevant behaviours include accountability to the parliament through the government, the need to behave with honesty and integrity, avoidance of conflict of interest, prohibition of the improper use of inside information or the employee's position to gain (or seek to gain) benefit or advantage for the employee or others, and the need to act with care and diligence. (As at 5 January 2016, section 4.10 of the Code of Conduct on the Australian Public Service Commission website had last been updated in August 2015, with a note that it may not reflect current legislation.)

Section 18 of the PGPAR makes it mandatory for an approval of relevant money to be recorded in writing as soon as practicable after it is given. The purpose of the provision is to lay down an evidentiary trail regarding the proposed expenditure. In this regard, RMG no. 400 (p. 11) cautions that 'the official should consider who is going to rely on the record and ensure that the record is proportionate to the significance, value, level of risk and sensitivities associated with the proposed commitment'. It is worth noting at this stage of the process that the approval needs to be consistent with the CPR clause 9.2 requirement that the estimated value of a procurement 'is the maximum value (including GST) of the proposed contract, including options, extensions, renewals or other mechanisms that may be executed over the life of the contract'.

Ethical behaviour and non-discrimination

Ethical behaviour and fair dealing make good business sense by engendering trust and allowing the parties to a transaction to minimise conflict and uncertainty.

Clauses 6.6 to 6.8 of the CPRs stipulate that ethical behaviour is mandatory for officials undertaking procurement. Relevant behaviours include dealing with actual, potential and perceived conflicts of interest; dealing equitably with potential suppliers, tenderers, and suppliers; complying with directions relating to gifts or hospitality, privacy principles and the *Crimes Act 1914*; equitable and non-discriminatory handling of complaints; and avoiding any benefit from dishonest unethical or unsafe supplier practices. In particular, contracts should not be entered into 'with tenderers who have had a judicial decision against them … relating to employee entitlements'.

Accountability and transparency

Accountability refers to the actions and decisions taken by officials, including outcomes, during the procurement process. The key requirement is that officials maintain a level of documentation commensurate with the scale, scope and risk of a procurement. CPR clause 7.2 specifies that concise and accurate information needs to be recorded about:

a. the requirement for the procurement;

b. the process that was followed;

c. how value for money was considered and achieved;

d. relevant approvals;

e. relevant decisions and the basis for those decisions.

Transparency refers to the steps taken by relevant entities to enable appropriate scrutiny of their procurement activity. The AusTender web-based facility www.tenders.gov.au is the key means for ensuring transparency. Clauses 7.7 and 7.8 of the CPRs states:

> each relevant entity must maintain on AusTender a current procurement plan containing a short strategic procurement outlook. The annual procurement plan should include the subject matter of any significant planned procurement and the estimated publication date of the approach to market. Relevant entities should update their plans regularly throughout the year.

Specific requirements for reporting on consultancies in Annual Reports were published on 29 May 2014 (but not apparently updated for the PGPA Act as at 5 January 2016).

Risk management

Managing risk is an essential aspect of project management. Overall risks of using a consultant should be considered as early as possible in the procurement process to maximise the opportunity for adopting mitigation strategies, if required. In the case of complex projects, it is worth seeking professional advice, or consulting older publications such as Purchasing Australia (1997) and Australian Government

Solicitor publications (AGS 1997a, 1997b). Although some aspects of these publications are now outdated (for example the procurement framework and policy) they still offer a range of practical advice.

As well as the risk of hiring a consultant, the project itself will involve risk. Good consultants will automatically assess the risks associated with a project, either as part of their proposal or once the contract has been signed. Clients should always ask for a risk assessment and the consultant's proposed method of dealing with risks. In the case of large or complex projects, it is a good idea to ask the consultant to produce a Project Charter or Plan, to ensure that both sides have an agreed understanding of both the content of the project, as well as who bears likely risks and implements appropriate mitigation strategies.

Not all risk is borne by the client. When considering how to bid for a project, a consultant will typically take into account a wide range of issues, including dependence on the client for the provision of data, the clarity of purpose demonstrated by the client (and hence risk of goal posts changing during the project), the continued availability of key staff (consultant's and client's), conflict of interest with other clients, the client's 'culture' (and hence the willingness to accept unconventional or 'creative' results), the realism of the client's estimate of the time required to complete the project, political factors beyond the consultant's control, profit levels, and whether the client will pay on time.

Both client and consultant risks are relevant to the success or failure of a project. As the client, you should endeavour to be aware of all of them.

Clauses 8.1 to 8.3 of the CPRs requires relevant entities to establish processes for the identification, analysis, allocation and treatment of risk when conducting a procurement, with the effort involved recommended to be commensurate with the scale, scope and risk of the project. The CPRs recommend that 'risks should be borne by the party best placed to manage them'. The Department of Finance (2014) has also released a Commonwealth Risk Management Policy which addresses action that needs to be taken at an entity level.

Table 1. Establishing the need for a consultant: Risks and mitigation strategies

Type of risk	Likely consequence	Mitigation strategy
Overlook or breach key provisions of AAIs, CPRs	• Decision to engage consultant is not compliant • Possible legal action, media interest, or probing by Senate Committees	• Read key documents, particularly AAIs for your agency • Check with procurements section or legal adviser • Check for existing or proposed whole-of-government procurement
Insufficient funding	• Purchase or availability of services delayed • Premature termination of contract • Reduced quality of output	• Ensure funds and appropriate delegations are available at the outset • Allow for contingencies and risk in contract • Allow for contingencies. 10 to 15 per cent of total contract value is often used in the commercial sector • Check that there are no follow-on costs after completion of the consultancy
Unrealistic timeframe for completion of task by consultant	• Delivery schedule not met • Lower quality product delivered • Bad reputation among consultants (and possibly higher quotes for next tender)	• Plan ahead • Where the timeframe is unavoidable, select a reputable consultant with large resource base
Realistic solution not feasible	• Unnecessary expenditure • On the other hand, external confirmation of the lack of a feasible solution may be an advantage • Finalisation of the project may be difficult	• Perform detailed needs analysis before the decision to hire a consultant • If it seems likely that a solution may not be found, provide in the contract for flexibility to terminate the contract
Misinterpretation of needs, or inability to use results	• Unnecessary expenditure • Failure to implement optimal policy outputs	• Specify clear deliverables • Check 'needs analysis' with stakeholders • Carry out a 'dry run' using dummy results to check how they will be used in practice (e.g. for policy advice, statistical testing) • Perform a 'gap analysis' to compare expected outputs of consultancy against what is needed for policy advice, etc.

Tips and traps

Users of consultancy services sometimes complain that consultants simply pump them for information and then sell it back to them. (The old joke is that a consultant is someone who borrows your watch, then charges you to tell you the time.) In some areas of government, it will be inevitable that consultants will need to learn enough about your business to be able to provide informed output. But a consultant may also take an inordinately long time to learn about your business. If this is the case, then review your perceived needs for consultancy services. Alternatively, review your selection processes.

It would be difficult to over-emphasise the point that clarity of purpose is essential to a successful consultancy project. If you are not sure what is really needed or how you will use the output, then it may be useful to first engage a consultant on a short-term basis to help you think through the issues. A good test is to ask whether you would be comfortable defending your justification for having hired a consultant in front of a Senate committee or an auditor.

There is an enduring myth in parts of the Australian Public Service that consultants will take any job thrown at them by any client. It may be true that a consultant will eventually be found to take on a badly defined or 'messy' task. But good consultants (who usually have more work than they can handle) will be highly unlikely to accept (or bid for) work that they suspect will involve unnecessary problems and conflicts. Failure by clients to clarify their needs and requirements in a business case can therefore limit the choice of consultants available to them, and may result in lower quality output.

Open tendering processes can be very useful in an unknown market where it is necessary to 'test the water'. However, they can involve significant cost to a client (time spent on selection processes) and consultants (preparation of bids). Because of the time and money required, many consultants try to avoid open tendering processes unless they believe that there is a reasonable chance of winning.

For a fixed price $100,000 tender, for example, a consultant might assume that there will be five or so serious bidders, including themselves. The chance of winning is only 0.2 per cent, so the expected value of the job is only $20,000. Taking into account time spent obtaining a briefing, thinking through the approach, doing some background research, writing the proposal, and the use of support staff to prepare it for submission, about three consulting days may be involved. The opportunity cost to a consultant with a daily charge-out rate of $1,200 would be about $3,600: a substantial reduction in profit if the bid were successful, and a straight loss if it were not. The net expected value is thus $16,400. At the charge-out rate of $1,200 per day, this represents 13.6 days of work. If consultants feel unable to complete the job within this time (including time spent on project management, travel, administration, etc.) they will probably not bid. (In some firms any loss would be deducted from the consultant's remuneration, or the consultant would need to make up any shortfall in hours spent on the project in their own time.)

If you expect to hire consultants reasonably frequently, panel arrangements may be worth considering, if they can better achieve value for money. Appointment of a number of good consultants with a broad range of skills saves time later because there is no need to repeat the tender and selection processes. You can then choose the best one to engage for a specific project, as required. Panel arrangements may also involve a fixed fee (often lower than normal if there is an expectation of continuing work) for the period of the panel. Multi-use lists are another possibility in that they establish a list of pre-qualified suppliers. But the establishment of multi-use lists is not in itself a procurement process. Suppliers who satisfy qualification requirements still need to be engaged through an 'approach to market'.

Where guaranteed access to a consultant is required, consider the possibility of a retainer fee. A retainer ensures that a consultant will make themselves available, if required, at no extra cost, although they may not be used at all if a need does not arise. A retainer fee has the advantage of being lower than normal rates because it provides the consultant with a definite stream of income, and the consultant is bound contractually to provide a specified amount of time (for example, three days per week) to the client, if required. On the other hand, if the consultant is not used very often, the total cost in terms of output may become unjustifiably high.

Where the objectives or likely scope of a project are difficult to determine with any certainty at the outset, a decision-tree approach may be appropriate. For example, the project could be structured to begin with a short feasibility and scoping study at a fixed price of $5,000. The scoping study would provide information to the client on likely cost (at least for the next stage), relevant analytical methodologies, and perhaps a refinement of the objectives. On this basis, the client might proceed to the next stage of data collection at a fixed price of, for example, $50,000. Further stages (such as data collation and interpretation, interviews with stakeholders, production of a report, and implementation of recommendations) could then be considered sequentially. The client retains the option at each stage to abort the project or to continue to the next stage. The advantage is that not all the resources need to be committed at the beginning, when uncertainty is still high. It also offers the potential advantage of being able to bring in different consultants for various stages, particularly where specialist skills are required. In effect, milestones become decision points. A potential disadvantage of staging a procurement is that clauses 9.2 to 9.6 of the CPRs require estimation of the combined maximum value of all the stages. Where estimation is not possible for the entire duration of the contract, the procurement must be treated as exceeding the relevant threshold (e.g. $80,000 for NCCEs).

An issue that may need to be addressed is the distinction between consultants and employees. If consultants are required to work closely with other staff on-site for lengthy periods, care will be needed to ensure that they do not, as a result, lose their status during the contract period as independent contractors to the extent that they could be regarded as employees. Because of the inherent legal complexities, it is advisable to seek legal advice prior to an approach to market.

If a consultant is engaged because specialist skills are not available in-house, a key consideration to address at the outset is the ability of the Commonwealth entity to select the most appropriate expert and how to manage the contract. One solution to the lack of in-house expertise is to obtain separate advice from a consultant in the same field. For example, a specialist academic economist or engineer could be hired to be part of the selection committee, or to provide advice on outputs during the course of the consultancy. The need for such external expertise should be determined on the basis of risk. If specialist knowledge is important in ensuring successful outputs, or if the consequences of unsuccessful outputs are significant, then the case for external advice is likely to be strong. Even if external advice is obtained, care is still required to ensure that the 'expert' selected is competent in the relevant area. Simply choosing a generalist economist or engineer may not be sufficient if highly specialised knowledge is required for a high-risk part of a project.

In some cases, it may be desirable or necessary to hire different specialist consultants, such as an economist and an engineer, to work on a single, specific problem. Some consulting firms can provide the whole range of different skills in-house. But it may also be the case that a tender process results in a choice of two different individual consultants or two different firms as the best outcome. In this situation it would be prudent in terms of risk management to have the two different parties sign a protocol that commits them to work collaboratively and cooperatively on the project.

If transfer of knowledge to your agency is a priority, ensure that you have sufficient staff to work with the consultant. Your staff need to have adequate skills to enable them to understand the issues, and will need to be readily available throughout the consultancy.

3

Preparing to approach the market

Some basics

Drafting request documentation (tenders, expressions of interest, etc.) is much easier if you are clear about what you need. Talking to someone who regularly engages consultants can also help one to understand the finer points of the procurement process and avoid pitfalls.

In particular, it always pays to check draft documentation with legal and probity advisers, or subject experts. For example, release of request documentation may in itself generate an obligation on the relevant entity, in the form of a so-called Process Contract. The relevant entity may be bound to observe the procedures (e.g. evaluation criteria or timelines) exactly as specified in the request documentation. Without a doubt, legal advice should be sought before the issue of any documents.

A word of caution is warranted; however, no set of dot points can adequately cover the full gamut of considerations involved in arranging a successful tender process. The need to ensure fair and ethical dealing, for example, can involve various unforeseen issues that may not be immediately obvious to even an experienced procurement official.

Although it may seem to involve unnecessary additional work, it is worthwhile during the preparatory stage to produce a rough outline plan or running sheet of the proposed procurement process, detailing the steps required, indicative timelines, resources needed, etc. Time spent considering such issues at an early stage can reduce risk and make life easier later, because some action taken now (or not taken) will affect the process in the future.

For example, if sufficient contingency time is not built into the planning process for checking legal aspects, any later unavailability of the relevant legal personnel (due perhaps to illness or other duties) may delay or impede required policy outcomes. Will there be someone available all the time to monitor and answer questions from potential suppliers on AusTender? Similarly, it is worth checking on the availability of members of the submission evaluation committee at an early stage, as well as checking that members are comfortable with the evaluation criteria before the approach to market.

An advantage that may not be immediately obvious is that drawing up a plan makes it easier to recall developments later, when preparing a written record of the procurement process. In other words, it can also be used as a memory-jogger, or even as a basic draft for reporting purposes.

Australian Government requirements

The 2014 Commonwealth Procurement Rules

There is no substitute for making oneself familiar with the detail of the Commonwealth Procurement Rules (CPRs) which replaced the 2005 Commonwealth Procurement Guidelines (CPGs) from 1 July 2014. The core principle of the CPRs is 'value for money', a concept that is explained in just over a page of Chapter 4 of the CPRs. In essence, 'value for money' does not just mean 'lowest cost'. Criteria such as the quality of the goods and services, the supplier's experience, and the fostering of competition, for example, provide sufficient flexibility in an evaluation process to enable an entity to choose a supplier that is likely to provide the best value for money.

The CPRs apply to Non-Corporate Commonwealth Entities (NCCEs) and to those Corporate Commonwealth Entities (CCEs) listed in section 30 of the *Public Governance, Performance and Accountability Rule 2014* (PGPAR).

The CPRs are neatly divided into two sections. Both divisions contain mandatory rules (identifiable by use of the word 'must' in bold text in a sentence) and so-called 'best practice' provisions that are generally identifiable by the use of the word 'should'. Relevant entities to which the CPRs apply must comply with the provisions of Division 1, regardless of procurement value.

If the procurement value exceeds a specified threshold, the rules in Division 1 must be followed, but the additional rules in Division 2 of the CPRs also apply. For example, Division 2 permits limited tenders only in certain circumstances (CPR clause 10.3). However, Appendix A of the CPRs also provides for a range of exemptions from Division 2 rules. Procurement of goods and services from a Small and Medium Enterprise (SME) with at least 50 per cent Indigenous ownership, procurement for providing foreign assistance, or for procuring government advertising services, are examples of exemptions.

For NCCEs, the procurement threshold is $80,000 (including GST) and for CCEs subject to the CPRs, it is $400,000 (including GST). There is also a threshold of $7.5 million for construction services (CPR clause 9.7), but these are not considered here.

It is also advisable to check the Resource Management Guides (RMGs) available on the Department of Finance website: www.finance.gov.au/resource-management/index. For example, with limited exceptions it is now mandatory for NCCEs to use the Commonwealth Contracting Suite (CCS) for procurements under $200,000 (including GST). However, RMG no. 420 also lists exceptions to this requirement; such as procurement of Information Communication Technology. In a number of other cases, use of the CCS is optional.

Ways of approaching the market

Three procurement methods are permitted under Chapter 9 (Division 1) of the CPRs:

1. *Open tender:* as the term suggests, an open tender is published and invites submissions in response from all interested potential suppliers. All open tenders must be advertised as an approach to market (ATM) on AusTender: www.tenders.gov.au (CPR clause 7.9).

2. *Pre-qualified tender:* a pre-qualified tender is published, but involves an invitation only to selected potential suppliers (CPR clause 9.9). Shortlisted potential suppliers who responded to an open approach to market on AusTender; those who were selected from a multi-use list using an open approach to market; and those with specific licences or who comply with a specific legal requirement, would qualify for this form of selection.

3. *Limited tender:* it is not uncommon for a relevant entity to approach one or more potential suppliers to make submissions. Where the procurement threshold is exceeded, however, the rules of Division 2 apply. If the threshold is exceeded, then under CPR clause 10.3, for example, a relevant entity may only use a limited tender where no submissions that represented value for money were received in an open approach to market, when only one business can supply goods or services (e.g. because of a patent), in cases of extreme urgency brought on by unforeseen events, etc.

Irrespective of which method is used to approach the market, or whether the procurement threshold is exceeded or not, the core requirement of achieving value for money must be satisfied. CPR clauses 4.4 and 4.5 outline relevant criteria.

Request documentation

It is now mandatory, with some exceptions, for NCCEs to use the CCS when purchasing goods or services valued under $200,000 (including GST). The CCS contains the Commonwealth Approach to Market Terms, the Commonwealth Contract Terms and the Commonwealth Purchase Order Terms, whose terms are non-negotiable.

In approaching the marketplace to obtain goods or services, it is obviously necessary to inform potential suppliers of the relevant entity's requirements. To ensure avoidance of ambiguity or misunderstanding, this information is transmitted through so-called request documentation. Clause 10.6 of the CPRs specifies that request documentation must include a complete description of:

a. the procurement, including the nature, scope and, when known, the quantity of the goods and services to be procured and any requirements to be fulfilled, including any technical specifications, conformity certification, plans, drawings, or instructional materials;

b. any conditions for participation, including any financial guarantees, information and documents that potential suppliers are required to submit;

c. any minimum content and format requirements;

d. evaluation criteria to be considered in assessing submissions; and,

e. any other terms or conditions relevant to the evaluation of submissions.

Confidential or security-sensitive information need not be released (CPR clauses 7.20 and 10.7), but the overarching principle is that potential suppliers are dealt with fairly and in a non-discriminatory manner. Requests for information must be addressed in a way that avoids giving an unfair advantage to any potential supplier or group. If evaluation criteria or specifications for goods and services are modified during the course of the procurement, for example, full information must be transmitted to all potential suppliers, and adequate time provided for modification of submissions.

Technical specifications must be based on international standards unless they fail to meet a relevant entity's requirements or would impose greater burdens than the use of recognised Australian standards. Request documentation must also not specify that potential suppliers have previous experience with the relevant entity or with the Australian Government or in a particular location. Chapter 10 of the CPRs details other conditions as well, including minimum time limits for the lodgement of submissions. It is sometimes the case that potential suppliers request or require that the content of their submissions remain confidential; that is, not released to the public.

Except for the successful tenderer, submissions must be kept confidential. Once a contract has been awarded, any claim by the successful supplier to confidentiality needs to be assessed by the relevant entity. According to CPR clause 7.22, 'the need to maintain the confidentiality of information should always be balanced against the public accountability and transparency requirements of the Australian Government'. For this reason it is prudent for request documentation to alert potential suppliers to government and parliamentary practice.

Relevant entities are required to give potential suppliers sufficient time to prepare and lodge submissions in response to an approach to market. The minimum time limit of 25 days specified in the CPRs may be shortened (clause 10.19) or extended (clause 10.20) in particular circumstances.

Workers' compensation insurance is compulsory in all states and territories of Australia. However, a risk assessment conducted in conjunction with a proposed procurement may indicate the desirability of a potential supplier also holding public liability, product liability, professional indemnity, general business, or other forms of insurance in order to minimise the risks borne by a relevant entity. Any requirements to hold insurance can be included in request documentation, with provision for specific confirmation by the potential supplier incorporated into the selection process.

A supplier's financial viability can deteriorate or improve quickly with changes to the economic or operating environment. It is therefore prudent to screen out high-risk potential suppliers. Request documentation should specify the documents that are required in submissions to undertake a financial viability assessment of potential suppliers. Tenderers can also be required to provide contact details for referees who can comment on the competence of an individual tenderer or the business history of the firm. Instances of past bankruptcy, and performance in fulfilling previous contracts, can also be used to assess reliability.

Unless already included in a draft contract, request documentation should also indicate that the contract will include clauses providing for payment to the supplier no later than 30 days after the date of receipt by the NCCE of a correctly rendered invoice (Department of Finance 2014, RMG no. 417). Under certain conditions, late payment by the NCCE involves a penalty of an interest payment on the outstanding amount.

The potential for unethical behaviour by a consultant is also worth exploring. Request documentation can be used in this regard by requiring contact details of referees and previous clients, with explicit advice that they may be contacted by officials. However, any adverse reports obtained from referees should be checked with legal advisers before use to ensure that natural justice principles are observed.

Officials should also heed CPR clause 6.7, which requires that:

> Relevant entities must not seek to benefit from supplier practices that may be dishonest, unethical or unsafe. This includes not entering into contracts with tenderers who have had a judicial decision against them (not including decisions under appeal) relating to employee entitlements and who have not satisfied any resulting order. Officials should seek declarations from all tenderers confirming that they have no such unsettled orders against them.

Once begun, a procurement process cannot be terminated if satisfactory submissions have been received, unless the agency determines that it is not in the public interest to continue (clause 10.31 of the CPRs). A contract must be awarded, provided that at least one of the tenderers meets the requirements of the approach to market, including the provision of value for money. The step of issuing request documentation is therefore one that warrants close attention.

Accountable Authority Instructions

A relevant entity's Accountable Authority Instructions (AAIs) are an essential starting point in preparing request documentation because they may contain entity-specific guidance or requirements that are additional to those in the CPRs.

Model AAIs are published by the Department of Finance in RMG no. 206 (for NCCEs) and RMG no. 213 (for CCEs). As their name suggests, they deal with the whole gamut of resource management issues relevant to Commonwealth entities, including procurement. Some relevant entities publish their AAIs, or at least the table of contents, online.

Commonwealth procurement-connected policies

Sections 15 and 21 of the PGPA Act require that procurement by NCCEs be conducted 'in a way that is not inconsistent with the policies of the Australian Government'. The Department of Finance RMG no. 415 provides guidance to Commonwealth entities on how approval is to be obtained to designate a policy as being procurement-related. Approvals lapse after five years, so it is important for officials undertaking procurements to check the currency of any policies.

The Department of Finance website provides a list of policies: www. dpmc.gov.au/indigenous-affairs/economic-development/indigenous-procurement-policy-ipp (accessed January 2016). With the exception of a Building Code requirement, the policies and associated policy departments listed on the Department of Finance website are shown in Table 2 below:

Table 2. Policies related to Commonwealth procurement

Policy	Description	Policy department
Indigenous procurement policy www.dpmc.gov.au/indigenous-affairs/about/jobs-land-and-economy-programme/ipp	Three per cent of Commonwealth entity contracts to be awarded to Indigenous businesses by 2020, within interim targets. In addition, certain contracts are to be set aside for Indigenous businesses, as well as other requirements.	Department of the Prime Minister and Cabinet IndigenousProcurement@pmc.gov.au
Workplace Gender Equality www.wgea.gov.au/about-wgea/workplace-gender-equality-procurement-principles	The Workplace Gender Equality Procurement Principles require entities to obtain a letter of compliance from certain tenderers (employers with 100 or more employees) indicating compliance with the *Workplace Gender Equality Act 2012*.	Department of Employment. Workplace Gender Equality Agency. wgea@wgea.gov.au
Australian Industry Participation (AIP) www.industry.gov.au/industry/IndustryInitiatives/AustralianIndustryParticipation/Pages/default.aspx	The AIP Framework applies to procurements of $20 million and more. Potential suppliers may be required to prepare and implement an Australian Industry Participation (AIP) plan.	Department of Industry and Science. Officials should check specific requirements with the Australian Industry Participation Policy Team aip@industry.gov.au

Under sections 22 and 93 of the PGPA Act, CCEs are only subject to policies of the Australian Government if directed by a government policy order issued by the Minister of Finance (see RMG no. 207). Before making an order, the Finance Minister must be satisfied that the minister responsible for the policy has consulted the CCE on its application as part of an effective consultation process. As at 15 June 2015, there were no government policy orders in effect: www.wgea.gov.au/about-legislation/workplace-gender-equality-procurement-principles (accessed January 2016).

Australia is a signatory to bilateral free trade arrangements with a number of countries. These arrangements are implemented domestically by legislation and/or Commonwealth policy. All relevant international obligations have been incorporated into the CPRs. According to CPR clause 2.14, 'an official undertaking a procurement is [therefore] not required to refer directly to international agreements'.

Competition is a key element of the Australian Government's procurement framework. It is mandatory under CPR clause 5.3 to avoid discrimination against potential suppliers 'due to their size, degree of foreign affiliation or ownership, location, or the origin of their goods and services'. In addition, officials are encouraged in CPR Chapter 5 to avoid requiring the preparation of costly submissions and other barriers to entry that would unfairly discriminate against SMEs. CPR clause 5.5 states that 'the Australian Government is committed to NCCEs sourcing at least 10 per cent of procurement by value from SMEs', but, as at January 2016, this did not appear to be a required procurement-connected policy.

Accountability and transparency

Parliamentary committees have in the past expressed concern and frustration about the apparent lack of transparency and accountability involved in procurement activity undertaken by Commonwealth entities.

A key feature of the CPRs (in particular, Chapter 7) is the emphasis on maintaining appropriate records during each phase of a procurement process. Officials are required 'to maintain for each procurement a level of documentation commensurate with the scale, scope and risk of the procurement. Documentation is expected to provide information on matters such as the requirement for the procurement, the process followed, how value for money was considered and achieved, and decisions taken. Documentation must be retained in accordance with the *Archives Act 1983*.

AusTender provides a convenient platform for maintaining records in a manner that is easily accessible to the public. Relevant entities are required to maintain a current procurement plan on AusTender, in order to provide advance notice to potential suppliers of their strategic procurement outlook. It is mandatory to publish all open tenders on AusTender, although it may also be used for pre-qualified and limited tender approaches to market.

A range of information must also be recorded on AusTender. Contracts above $10,000 (including GST) concluded by NCCEs (and $400,000 for prescribed CCEs), and any amendments must be entered on AusTender within 42 days of execution. Mandatory Chapter 7 requirements also apply to standing offers, provision on request of information about sub-contractors, disclosure of procurements in annual reports, disclosure of non-compliance with the CPRs, etc. Officials are also encouraged to 'alert potential suppliers to the public accountability and transparency requirements of the Australian Government, including disclosure to the Parliament and its committees'. Contracts should enable the Australian National Audit Office (ANAO) to access a supplier's records and premises to carry out appropriate audits; reflected in clause C.C.20 of the CCS.

With limited exceptions, use by NCCEs of the CCS (RMG no. 420) is mandatory for procurements below $200,000 (including GST). The suite codifies some of the accountability and transparency requirements. For example, the Commonwealth Contract Terms include provisions dealing with supplier compliance with Commonwealth laws and policies, ranging from record keeping, access for the ANAO, Indigenous procurement policy, etc.

Under the so-called 2001 Murray Motion, the Senate of the Australian Parliament imposes an additional transparency requirement in the form of a Senate Order. The Order requires each NCCE to develop an internet listing twice a year that identifies contracts entered into during the preceding calendar or financial year, valued at or above $100,000 (GST inclusive), along with details relating to each of those contracts. On the basis of subsequent amendments, the Department of Finance now publishes the reports on AusTender on behalf of NCCEs. However, ministers are still required to table in the Senate letters of advice that the NCCEs that they administer have placed a list on the internet. RMG no. 403 provides a letter template as well as detailed administrative information regarding the Senate Order. Letters must be tabled within two months of the end of the reporting period to which they refer.

Finally, accountable authorities are required by sections 19 and 91 of the PGPA Act (and clause 7.24 of the CPRs) to provide an annual report on compliance (and non-compliance) with the PGPA framework. The report must be provided to the Finance Minister as well as the entity's responsible minister. Detailed requirements are set out in the Department of Finance (2015) RMG no. 208.

Tips and traps

- Lack of clarity may lead the successful tenderer to seek profitable variations once the contract has been signed and the client begins to specify 'additional' needs. Such **variations can be expensive**, so don't begrudge time spent on preparing a procurement plan and the request documentation. If it is not clear what additional work might be required, it is best to include in the request documentation 'options' for such work, and to ask for separate quotes for it. Options should form part of the final contract.

- There are no hard and fast rules, but **a statement of requirements of between one and three pages** of information may be suitable for straightforward consultancies. Background material in particular will enable consultants to see the bigger picture and help them prepare proposals that are ultimately of more benefit to the client.

- A long list of **evaluation criteria** can complicate the selection process unnecessarily. Consultants will need to provide lengthier bids, so that more time is spent by officials in reading and understanding submissions. The effort involved in documenting the evaluation committee's assessments against the criteria also increases.

- Too many evaluation criteria can also dissuade consultants from bidding. In one case, an agency listed over 30 selection criteria, many of them partially repetitive. Although the job was a six-figure one, a large firm decided not to bid because it was not confident that it could recover the estimated four weeks of work involved in preparing a proposal. **Framing an appropriate number of evaluation criteria** in a logical order, with minimum duplication, assists tenderers to present better submissions. It also makes it easier for you in the selection process stage. So don't skimp on time spent drawing up the evaluation criteria.

- Selection committees can save time and effort by signalling their needs with respect to the **length of submissions**. For example: 'We expect proposals to be no longer than about five to seven pages ... (excluding attachments such as CVs)'. Agencies that are significantly more prescriptive than this (for example, by specifying the exact number of pages, font size, etc.) are likely to reduce the field of bidders. Like most people, consultants prefer to work in an environment that is not overly directive or restrictive. Except for the marginal operators, many consultants are not so desperate for work that they will bid for jobs if they think that working with a particular agency will be a frustrating experience. So don't send the wrong signals in your tender documents.

- Preparing a bid costs money. Most consultants won't mind responding to a tender if they know that there is **a reasonable chance** of winning the job. Apart from the fact that tenders should always be fair, entities that frustrate bidders are likely to receive fewer bids in the longer term. This is not an academic point: some top-tier firms have in the past avoided bidding for jobs tendered by certain government agencies.

- Many experienced consultants are less keen to respond to open tenders because of the low expected value (probability of winning, multiplied by contract value) to them. An alternative is to first seek **Expressions of Interest** (EOI) as part of an open tender process. A response to an EOI requires less work than a tender submission, so that a larger field of consultants can be attracted. Only the shortlisted ones will subsequently face the cost of submitting a full proposal.

- Many consultants will not bid if they have tendered unsuccessfully several times with specific agencies. If your aim is to maintain a **pool of interested consultants** who have a knowledge of your area (to avoid becoming overly dependent on one supplier), then each must have a reasonable probability, but no certainty, of winning any specific tender. One consultant's rule of thumb is that, unless his firm wins at least one out of three invitations to tender, it refuses to incur further tendering costs in the future.

- It is possible to **signal an entity's requirements** without necessarily restricting the field of bidders. For example, if an agency places a premium on minimising the risk of disruption to a project due to departure or illness of consulting staff, then request documentation should mention this, and use a formulation something like: 'We expect that the successful tenderer will have satisfactory back-up arrangements to cover any loss of project staff'. This approach does not exclude small or specialist firms (which can form a contingency partnership with other consultants), but does signal a preference for a consultant with readily available back-up staff or ready access to expertise. Where there is a genuine need for urgent personal access to a consultant, it may be possible to specify a response time, or a requirement for face-to-face discussion, but care is required to avoid discriminating against non-local and foreign firms.

- Considerable leverage is available to a government agency at the stage of issuing request documentation, and prior to acceptance of a bid. Good use can be made of this in areas which do not directly affect the integrity of the procurement process. NCCEs can, for example, seek to negotiate additional conditions in the **draft contract** for jobs that exceed $200,000. Willingness to negotiate provides a useful signal of the flexibility and responsiveness of potential suppliers.

- Should the **likely** budget for the consultancy be revealed in the request documentation?

  - Despite the additional work imposed on the public service official, it is probably preferable in most cases to devote resources to better specifying the entity's requirements. (A consultant can be hired to assist with this, if necessary.) Clearly specified requirements will allow competent consultants to better gauge the extent of work required.

  - Consultants argue that, because their bids are based primarily on expected cost, a budget provides an indication of the scope of the job (in terms of consulting days allocated to it). A more realistic proposal—better suited to the client's needs—can be prepared if at least an indicative budget is known. Without any knowledge of the likely value of the project, it is argued, consultants may make very different assumptions about the extent and quality of the work required. Valid comparisons between those bidding then become all but impossible, it is argued. For example, it would be difficult to compare bids from two consultants, one of whom assumed that a project would be worth $500,000, and the other assumed a smaller job of about $40,000 in value. At least an order of magnitude 'ballpark figure' is required.

  – Some officials, however, point out that making the likely budget known beforehand invariably results in virtually all the tenderers quoting much the same price. It is always possible that a highly suitable bidder would have bid much lower because of their existing knowledge or skills. On the other hand, most experienced consultants will have similar views about the cost of a job, as long as a detailed specification is provided in the request documentation.

  – Further, public servants, particularly when they do not have a good knowledge of the market, can seriously under- or over-estimate the value of a project or the extent of work required. One apocryphal anecdote recounts an instance where the value of a project was grossly underestimated. After the project had been expanded to many times its original value, the client finally began to suspect that the consultant (who was relatively far more experienced in the field) had known all along what the value would eventually be, but had put in a very low initial bid to win the contract because of his strong expectation of an increase in scope after commencement.

  – A possible compromise is to make known a fairly broad range (say $50,000 to $80,000) to signal the expected order of magnitude of the contract, without diminishing too much the scope for price competition. However, even this approach may be flawed, unless the client is reasonably knowledgeable about consulting in the subject area or has access to some prior industry advice.

• Apart from probing to gain an insight into the likely budget, consultants will normally be interested in finding out about issues like the underlying or background reasons for the consultancy, the nature and strength of the business case for letting the consultancy, the likely overall scope of work, the amount of support or assistance that the agency envisages as its contribution to the project, the extent to which innovative methodologies or ideas are expected (they cost more than 'vanilla solutions'), the formal and informal decision-making processes within the organisation, and the likelihood that a report or other output will actually be implemented. As well as clear tender specifications, **face-to-face meetings** in the form of industry briefings are usually the best means for presenting such information, because discussion is possible. But don't forget to record the outcomes and to circulate them formally to attendees.

- Don't forget about the **implications of the GST**. Unless the bidder is registered for GST, your agency will not be able to claim a GST input tax credit for the consultancy fee paid. To maximise cash-flow benefits to your agency, the contract should specify that GST tax invoices are to be issued by the consultant as soon as any payment is due.

- Despite the extra cost involved, a high risk project may warrant the use of a specialist **peer reviewer** to provide confidence in the final product. If it is intended to use a specialist academic or consultant as a peer reviewer, this should be made known in tender documentation to avoid surprises. If a peer reviewer is used, it is also desirable that they be involved from the outset of the project. Peer review at the end of the project may result in disagreement about the quality or validity of outcomes. There is little or no scope for resolution at the stage of finalisation of a project. It is also important that the reviewer work to the entity's project manager; not to the consultant.

- Ownership of **intellectual property** (if any) that is developed during a project should be addressed clearly in the contract.

- Before issuing request documentation, undertake a **sanity check**: would you bid for this work if you were a good consultant who was not desperate for work?

Exhibit 3.1. Consider the following *before* issuing the request documentation

- The clarity of the requirement; it sometimes helps to specify what is *not* required.
- Does the request documentation allow for (rather than discourage) innovative solutions or approaches? Where possible, avoid specifying inputs or analytical approaches; focus on the output or outcome required.
- Is it (inadvertently) written around the capabilities of an identifiably specific consultant (not a good look)?
- Does the draft contract contain clauses that provide sufficient flexibility to alter specified outputs (but without changing the underlying nature of the tender process)?
- Will you be able to judge quality of output? How? You may need to specify existing technical standards (such as the Commonwealth Style Guide) in the contract. Is a peer reviewer desirable?
- The timeframe specified: officials often underestimate the time required to complete work, and consultants may take more time than either party expected.
- Are your specified outputs really important? It can add to costs if you over-specify your needs. Are your outputs and outcomes consistent with your initial Business Case proposing the procurement?
- Have you given your agency's legal and probity advisers or procurement manager enough time to check the documentation?
- Consistency of the project with relevant Australian Government policies; not just those listed in the Department of Finance (2015) RMG no. 415.
- Under the CPRs (clause 10.24) there is no discretion to accept late tenders, unless the tender is late solely because of the agency's own mishandling. If you are using a tender box, make sure that it is emptied exactly at the time specified. Access to a verifiable time-keeping device is essential, and witnesses are always useful.

Table 3. Preparing tender documentation: Risks and mitigation

Type of risk	Likely consequence	Mitigation strategy
Failure to specify all relevant contract requirements in request documentation	• Possible need to re-seek tenders or negotiate with winning tenderer	• Consult legal and probity advisers at an early stage before issuing documentation • Possibly allow industry expert to preview requirements • Draft documents to provide ability to vary conditions • Draft documents to provide ability to abort process at any time
Failure to conform to Commonwealth Procurement Rules (CPRs)	• Project attracts incommodious interest from parliamentary committees or ANAO • Accountable Authority must provide a non-compliance report to the Finance Minister	• Consult legal and probity advisers early in the process, particularly for complex procurements • Check with legal and probity advisers before any non-standard action such as acceptance of late submissions • Ensure completion of non-compliance report
Biased or unclear specification of requirements	• Claims of unethical or unfair dealing • Possible legal action • Limited response from potential tenderers • Loss of time in the long-term	• Use functional and performance specifications and criteria • Check with legal and probity advisers • Establish submission evaluation committee to check request documentation, including evaluation criteria, prior to issue • In complex cases, engage a consultant to help define or refine request documentation
Terms and conditions which are unattractive to suppliers	• Loading of costs on offers • Absence of submissions • Highly qualified offers • Legal action after commencement of contract • Costly disputes	• Check with the market before formal tender process • Investigate possibilities for sharing risk • Require tenderers to warrant in their submissions that they have assessed risks and allowed for them in tender price

Type of risk	Likely consequence	Mitigation strategy
Inadequate information provided or failure to answer suppliers' queries	• Claims of unethical behaviour, favouritism or unfair practices • Lack of bids • Higher quoted costs or qualified offers • Loss of time in long-term	• Develop a probity plan that includes quality control measures for dissemination of information and for ensuring its accuracy • Additional information provided to any tenderer should be distributed as soon as possible to others • Advise *all* potential tenderers of *all* responses to *all* queries received (but respect confidentiality) • Specify in request documentation the entity's designated staff for all contact with bidders • For separate briefings, ensure that another official is present (even for telephone conversations: use the loudspeaker facility) • Record on file all separate briefings provided, including all telephone conversations
Premature contractual commitment	• Tenderer(s) claim existence of a preliminary or implied contract • Legal action to recover costs from agency	• Avoid encouraging tenderer to begin work in anticipation of award of contract • In staged contracts, avoid giving the consultant working on the current stage any impression or promise of follow-on to the next stage
Breach of commercial confidentiality	• Claims of unethical behaviour, favouritism or unfair practices • Possible legal action	• Develop clear procedures for receipt, registration, storage, opening, filing, and handling of offers • If using a tender box, all offers kept sealed and secure until designated opening time • Staff access to documents on a 'need to know basis' • Request documentation makes clear what is considered to be confidential, including contract conditions
Consultant technically becomes an employee	• Increased legal responsibility • Increased cost	• Check with legal adviser where contract is being extended, on-site facilities are made available, consultant carries out investigation on behalf of Australian Government, leave periods are approved by the agency, etc.

Type of risk	Likely consequence	Mitigation strategy
Change to procedures or conditions specified in request documentation	• Potential breach of process contract • Legal action against entity, or ministerial representations	• Consider contents of request documentation carefully prior to issue • Check request documentation with legal adviser • If change is required after issue, consult probity adviser and ensure fair and equal treatment of all tenderers
Discriminatory selection process	• Breach of process contract • Legal action against entity, or ministerial representations	• Compliance with CPRs, especially Chapter 5 • Regard for competitive neutrality principles when dealing with a government business entity. www.finance.gov.au/archive/publications/finance-circulars/2004/01.html (accessed January 2016)

4

Fees and expenses

Some basics

There is no magic formula for determining the level of fees that will provide 'value for money'. Hence the need for competitive bidding as an indicator of 'market price'.

Large, established firms are likely to charge more. But the trade-off is that they may be able to respond better to any problems that arise during the project, so that overall risk to the government agency is reduced (although they may charge extra for solutions). This may not be apparent from the bid (submission) itself, but should be taken into account in gauging value for money.

On the other hand, small consulting firms may be more responsive to client needs than large ones. They are less likely to try to sell a pre-packaged approach or solution. Assuming the same level of skill as larger firms, they may therefore provide better value for money. However, they may represent a greater risk in terms of availability of personnel and ability to meet unforeseen needs and problems.

Fees can provide a lever for influencing a consultant's performance. A graduated, incentive-based scale that reflects differing degrees of performance is better than an 'all or nothing' penalty approach.

Payment schedules should be based on carefully defined and specific milestones. Of particular importance is that the milestones are easily measurable. Smaller firms may need more frequent milestones to ensure adequate cash flow for their continued operation.

If consultants are not registered for GST, then the entity that hires them will not be able to claim an input tax credit for the fee paid. To maximise cash-flow benefits to the entity, the contract should specify that tax invoices will be required for any payment to the consultant, unless they prefer not to obtain an Australian Business Number (ABN).

In some cases, it may be difficult to specify clearly the extent or quality of work required. Providing a ballpark figure (maximum, or a range) for the value of a job in tender documentation can 'signal' bidders to compete primarily on quality, with less emphasis on cost. Value for money is encouraged because excessively expensive bids, as well as superficial proposals, are avoided without eliminating price competition entirely.

Travel and accommodation expenses are usually charged at cost at non-Senior Executive Service (SES) rates. Consultants do not normally receive a travelling allowance, so the contract should specify that expenses are to be acquitted on the basis of receipts. A further possibility is to place a contractual cap on total expenses, in order to minimise costs.

Various payment arrangements are possible. Shenson (1990, Chapter 9) identifies a number, including the following:

- *Daily or hourly fee*: there is little incentive for the consultant to minimise the time spent on the job and the client bears all the risk.
- *Fixed-price fee*: the consultant bears the risk and is likely to have allowed a contingency margin in the bid, although it is unlikely to be apparent to the client. In an arrangement of this kind, it is important to have well-defined outputs.
- *Fixed fee plus expenses*: the most common form of contract used in the Australian Public Service. While the consultant bears the risk for the fixed fee, the client bears the risk of expenses unless the contract specifies that expenditure for expenses is subject to prior approval.

- *Fixed-price plus incentive*: if a special condition is met (for example, early delivery) an additional pre-specified fee may be paid to the consultant. An alternative form is to base the fee on an estimate by the consultant, for example $50,000, with a capped fixed price of $70,000. It can be agreed that any costs above the $50,000 threshold (but not exceeding $20,000) will be borne by the client at a rate such as 75 per cent, and the remainder by the consultant. This approach provides an incentive to the consultant to minimise costs above $50,000, but without necessarily compromising the quality or extent of the contract outputs.

- *Graduated incentive fee*: if the consultant estimates that the contract will require $50,000 of work, a range of $20,000 can be set on either side. The consultant may be required, for example, to bear 25 per cent of costs above $50,000 up to a maximum of $70,000. Similarly, the consultant may receive 50 per cent of any savings below the estimated project cost of $50,000.

- *Fixed-price with re-determination*: Where the scope and nature of the work is very vague, the parties may agree to proceed for a fixed fee to a defined milestone, by when the requirements will have been better defined and a fixed fee for the remainder of the work can be agreed.

- *Cost contract*: where the consultant will acquire technology or knowledge which can be used to earn profits elsewhere, it may be possible for the client to agree to pay some portion of the consultant's costs, but no fee (to reflect the revenue potential of the technology). This approach may be suitable for dealing with intellectual property.

Australian Government requirements

Apart from the broad provisions of the *Public Governance, Performance and Accountability Act 2013* regarding the 'proper use' of Commonwealth resources (see Chapter 2), obtaining 'value for money' is the primary guidance provided to government agencies of relevance to consulting services.

Contract fees may be affected by the extent of liability accepted by, or imposed on, the contractor. In general, liability should generally rest with the party best placed to minimise the occurrence of an identified risk, and any limitation of a contractor's liability should be based on comprehensive risk management.

Tips and traps

- Public servants are sometimes not aware of the fact that consultants normally consider time spent in **meetings with the client** to be **billable**. If the contract specifies that a certain number of consulting days (usually taken as 7.5 hours per day) will be spent on the project, then any anticipated meeting time should be taken into account in setting the budget for the project. Top-tier firms will not normally bill for time spent travelling to a meeting unless **travel** occurs during business hours and precludes the consultant from undertaking other work, but air and taxi fares and accommodation are considered to be legitimate expenses to be reimbursed by the client. (Consultants are generally reimbursed at non-SES rates. Unlike some public servants, they do not normally receive a daily travelling allowance.) Items such as **faxes** sent to clients, **telephone calls**, use of **couriers** and other out-of-pocket expenses are also considered to be expenses that are recoverable from the client. And don't forget to allow for time spent on project **management** tasks or the use of **materials** (printing multiple copies of reports can be expensive). Because practice differs widely between consultants, it is worth checking on each bidder's charging policy for all of these 'pass-through cost' items. Bidders are likely to be more accommodating if you do so in the request documentation.

- Whether you should **expect to pay a fee** each time that you deal with a consultant depends to a large extent on your relationship. There are no hard and fast rules, but the following provides some general guidance:
    - If you want to test the feasibility of a project and phone a consultant to 'pick their brains' in a general way, they will normally treat the enquiry as part of their marketing activity. But the consultant is likely to follow up in a few days to see if you want some work done. So be careful not to raise undue expectations during the first query.

- Frequent calls for (free) opinions to a tax consultant, on the other hand, would probably come to be seen as unwelcome if no paid work flowed from the queries.

- Asking a consultant for a 'one-page outline' on how to deal with an issue is likely to be seen in the context of a proposal. A 'proposal' comes closer to generating an expectation that work is available. It is worth making clear that you are still only in the stage of considering the possibilities. Except in very large projects, proposals may be provided free, although consultants themselves will consider whether it is worth their while preparing them for a specific enquirer. Unless you offer definite work, however, do not expect a full analysis that solves your problem.

- Once you ask a consultant to put together a proper plan (even a few pages), you start to cross the line into making serious use of a consultant's expertise and time and a fee should be expected. Caution is therefore required to avoid entering into an implicit contract, without considering fully the need for a consultant and the need for a tender process.

• Some agencies appear to select consultants purely on the basis of quoted cost, apparently avoiding larger firms. Unless all factors, including quality of output, are taken into account, the chance of obtaining **value for money, the primary consideration**, will be diminished.

• Where project outcomes are not entirely certain, or there is some likelihood that the analysis may point to further work, consider allowing for a **contingency amount** of, say, 10 to 15 per cent of the total project budget as part of the estimate of expected value of the procurement under CPR clause 9.2. Note that CPR clause 9.6 states that 'when the maximum value of a procurement over its entire duration cannot be estimated the procurement **must** be treated as being valued above the relevant procurement threshold'.

• Most consultants try to remain **competitive**. If consultants refuse to lower their fee in a competitive situation, their **quote** is likely to be fairly realistic for the proposed level of quality and time spent. If you are still not happy with it, ask an experienced colleague for advice, or even ask another firm (but be careful about commercial confidentiality). Alternatively, explore the possibility of reducing the scope of the work if budgetary considerations are of concern.

A refusal to accept a lower fee may be an indication of a good consultant who is in demand and can earn that fee elsewhere. And if a consultant does accept a fee that is lower than they wish, they may later cut corners to ensure they do not make a loss.

- Government entities sometimes seek to reduce risk to themselves by specifying a **fixed-price contract**. However, establishing the price in a reasonably competitive market means that the consultant is likely to insist on keeping strictly to the scope of the work defined in the contract, because there is little margin to adjust without incurring a loss. A client may therefore gain more certainty regarding the final amount to be paid to the consultant, but may bear a commensurately higher risk in terms of output if changes to the scope of the work are found to be required during the project. Because most projects require some adjustment as they proceed, neither side is likely to end up being entirely happy with the final outcome. Potential problems can be reduced, however, by ensuring clarity of requirement in the request documentation. Alternatively, provide in the contract for the ability to agree easily on changes to work specified. Such potential changes should be expressed in the form of options to ensure that they form part of the initial contract.

A major area of frustration to consultants is the **unavailability of data or personnel promised by clients**. The assumption that data are available is likely to be a significant factor in the framing of a bid: collection of original data is usually expensive. If there is any uncertainty about the quality or availability of data, bidders should be invited to inspect it for themselves as part of the tendering process, rather than specifying in request (tender) documentation that data will be made available. Similarly, if bidders were promised a contribution of personnel to help with the project, you need to make sure that they are available at the times when they are needed. If you do not make available data, staff, or other resources promised during the tender process, you should expect to meet any expenses incurred by the consultant in making up the shortfall. Delays are also likely.

Table 4. Fees and expenses: Risks and mitigation

Type of risk	Likely consequence	Mitigation strategy
Fee is too low	Consultant loses incentive to produce quality or timely output Possible request for renegotiation during contract	Fair negotiation of fees, possibly 'fixed price plus incentives' version Include options for additional work in contract Periodic review during contract Build a contingency allowance into the budget for the contract
Insufficient provision for expenses	Budget overrun for entity Lower quality output; reduced value for money	Request estimate of expenses over life of project as part of the submission Specify that only written variations to contract can result in extra expense Periodic review during contract Build a contingency allowance into entity's budget for the contract Contract should specify expense reimbursement only on basis of receipts Cap on expenses in contract
Fees or expenses too high	Reduced value for money	Encourage competitive bidding Develop strong working relationship with consultant from the outset to encourage fair dealing (and possible refund) Request cost breakdown with all invoices (including record of hours worked)

5

Choosing the consultant

Some basics

Choosing consultants is analogous to a staff selection process:

- Interview the short-listed bidders to provide an opportunity to probe claims and methodology. But make sure that it is the nominated team that is interviewed as part of a consultant's presentation, not just one of the firm's 'professional presenters'. The box below ('quick-check questions') provides a useful basis for discussion during the consultant's presentation.

- For large contracts, consider having an outsider sit on the evaluation committee, both for probity and to gain an external perspective; preferably someone from an agency with relevant expertise. Even an industry person not connected with the bidder can be used, but first seek agreement from all bidders, in case of a potential breach of any confidentiality provisions in their bids. For probity, external advisers need to sign confidentiality and conflict of interest declarations.

- Compare candidates only against the evaluation criteria set out in the request documentation.

- Interview referees, consult peers, or others who may have worked with the consultant. And don't just ask if everything was okay. Ask for examples of things that went well, *as well as* things that did not. Are the same personnel still involved?

- Don't promise the job to anyone before a final decision has been made.
- Provide debriefing for unsuccessful candidates.

Some degree of subjective or professional judgement will inevitably be required, but the primary evaluation should be carried out as objectively as possible against the evaluation criteria set out in the tender documentation. One of the reasons for the successful action against Airservices Australia by Hughes Aircraft Systems International was the failure by its predecessor organisation (the Civil Aviation Authority) to evaluate tenders in accordance with the priorities and methodology specified in the Request for Tender (AGS 1997a, 1997b).

If considered desirable, clarification of terms or outputs can be achieved through discussion after the receipt of submissions. The best results can be achieved before selection of a preferred bidder, but ethics demand that discussions should not merely be a means of playing bidders off against each other. In complex cases, use of trained negotiators is advisable. Prior legal and probity advice should be sought in any case, to avoid inadvertent breaches of contract law. Where none of the submissions received is considered to be satisfactory, an option is to relet the tender.

Exhibit 5.1. Questions to ask during a consultant's bid presentation

- What do you regard as our principal need or problem?
- Can you please analyse for us the principal strengths and weaknesses of your proposed approach/methodology?
- What alternative methodologies could be used? (As a check on whether the consultant will only apply preconceived ideas or proprietary 'packages'.)
- What specifically can you offer us that others cannot?
- How will we measure or evaluate your success in meeting our needs?
- What related experience have you (the actual personnel nominated, not the firm as a whole) had in working with similar organisations, or with other organisations in this industry or field?
- What assurances can you offer on the availability of nominated personnel?
- How do you plan to maintain communication with our contact officer?
- What related experience have you had in working on similar issues?
- If you plan to use sub-contractors, what are the arrangements?
- From your (consultant's) point of view, what are the major risks in the project, and what strategies do you intend to adopt to mitigate them? What risks do you see facing us (the client)?

- Can you confirm that your stated fees (*and* expenses) are likely to represent all costs to be incurred? If expenses are based on cost recovery, then what is the likely overall expense to be incurred? Do you propose to charge for meeting time, time spent travelling, telephone calls, taxis, etc.?
- Do all quoted costs and fees include GST?
- What penalties should be imposed on you for under-performance or late delivery?
- What other work do you have in hand at the moment? Do you have the capacity to meet the timeframe specified?
- How do you propose to work with our nominated resources (where some of the client's staff will be working on the project alongside the consultant)?
- What quality assurance procedures do you have? What procedures do you have in place to ensure that files are maintained adequately?
- Do you have any conflict of interest (name a few obvious parties to provide a prompt), and how will you handle this situation?

Source: Adaptation and expansion of list in Shenson (1990: 47).

Australian Government requirements

Evaluation of value for money offered by submissions should be on a whole-of-life basis, taking into account factors relevant to the project under consideration. Costs and benefits should be compared on a common basis over time, including through the calculation of 'equivalent annual value' rather than net present value, where appropriate.

Entities can claim GST input tax credits for services provided, but only if the consultant is registered for GST purposes. This may be a relevant consideration in the case of individual consultants or community groups.

Chapter 4 of the CPRs lists factors other than cost that should be taken into account in assessing value for money.

Confidentiality during the tendering process

'In the Hughes Aircraft case ... one of the breaches of the tender process identified by Finn J was breach of confidentiality. Information about the bidders' prices was provided by the Civil Aviation Authority Board to the portfolio minister and to personnel from another department, including the permanent head and minister of that department. Finn J had no doubt that passing on this information to personnel (including the minister) from the other department was a breach of the strict confidentiality which was part of the package of terms of the request for tender. The department's role was to assess the Australian Industry Involvement commitments of the two bids and providing the prices to that department was irrelevant to that task.

Providing that information to the portfolio minister also constituted a breach of confidentiality in the circumstances. This was because the information was, as it were, volunteered by the Board rather than requested by the minister. Finn J was in no doubt that the minister ... could have made a direction to the Board to provide the information ... But this [legislative] power had not been used.'

Source: Seddon (2004: 320).

Debriefing

Clause 7.15 of the CPRs states that:

> following the rejection of a submission or the award of a contract, officials must promptly inform affected tenderers of the decision. Debriefings must be made available, on request, to unsuccessful tenderers outlining the reasons the submission was unsuccessful. Debriefings must also be made available, on request, to the successful supplier(s).

Clause 6.8 of the CPRs further advises that:

> if a complaint about procurement is received, relevant entities must apply equitable and non-discriminatory complaint-handling procedures. Relevant entities should aim to manage the complaint process internally, when possible, through communication and conciliation.

The gun buy-back scheme

Following the tragic events at Port Arthur in Tasmania in April 1996, the Australasian Police Ministers' Council met and agreed to a 10-point plan for the regulation of firearms on a national basis.

The advertising and public relations contract for the Gun Buy-Back campaign was the subject of a tender process. The responsible agency, the Office of Government Information and Advertising (OGIA), in consultation with, among other agencies, the Attorney-General's Department, developed a list of potential tenderers from its register of consultants. However, the name of another advertising firm was added on the basis of 'a facsimile from the then Chief Political Adviser to the Prime Minister, which suggested inclusion of DDB Needham, Adelaide.' (para. 3.142)

'OGIA advised the ANAO that the decision to include DDB Needham on the shortlist … was made with the agreement of the evaluation committee … [but] neither OGIA or the Attorney-General's Department were able to provide the ANAO with adequate written evidence documenting the committee decision.' (paras 3.155, 3.156)

The ANAO concluded that it 'considers that adequate documentation of decisions helps to ensure transparency and accountability. … A tangible management trail provides protection for all concerned, including those who may have to take decisions later in the process but who … may not have been involved in the early stages of decision-making or assessment.' (para. 3.159)

Source: ANAO (1997).

Tips and traps

- Departmental registers and AusTender can provide useful information about previous work done for the department by consultants. However, if use is made of any remarks about a consultant's previous work then the principles of natural justice require that the consultant be given an opportunity to comment on them. If using a **'consultants register'**, check whether the same personnel are being proposed again by the consultant, and whether the nature of the job is comparable to previous work carried out for the Department.

- Avoid accepting **hospitality** or favours during a tender selection process, including seemingly innocuous offerings such as a cup of coffee in a coffee shop. Even if there is a long-established relationship with a bidder, or the hospitality is part of another project, probity demands not only impartiality but also the need to avoid being *seen* to be compromised in any way.

- In some entities, the **preferred bidder** has in the past been announced publicly before finalisation of the contract. Where the preferred bidder is made known, it may significantly reduce the agency's scope for further negotiation of terms and conditions with that bidder. If negotiations fall through, the scope for negotiations with alternative bidders is also diminished.

- Some bidders may seek to present their bid at an interview by using specialised presenters who are not part of the consultant's project team. Such **presentations** can be a waste of time, particularly if the presenters are not familiar with the issues or the methodology to be used. Nor is the client afforded the opportunity of meeting the people who will actually carry out the work. *Insist on the actual team of nominated personnel making the presentation.* Apart from getting to know them, you will be better able to assess their capabilities.

- Large consulting firms may cite as part of their **'previous history and experience'** work which has been done within the firm, but in other cities by people other than those nominated in the proposal. The implication is that the experience is available within the firm and can be drawn on if required. Take the time to ask during the presentation about the personal involvement of the team nominated in the proposal in the projects cited. If none of the nominated personnel were personally involved, ask how the firm's experience will be drawn on for your own project.

- Entities do not have discretion to accept **late tenders**, unless the tender is late solely because of the agency's own mishandling. All suppliers must meet a common deadline.

Table 5. Choosing the consultant: Risks and mitigation

Type of risk	Likely consequence	Mitigation strategy
Bidders not treated equally	• Loss of confidence by suppliers in entity processes • Ministerial representations • Possible legal action • Non-compliance report required	• Check before selection process commences that all tenderers received the same request documentation: if necessary, rectify, seek legal and probity advice, and consider need to reopen tenders • Check all records of conversation in case of need to correct information provided, or to provide identical information to all bidders
Premature contract created	• Loss of confidence by suppliers in entity processes • Ministerial representations • Possible legal action • Non-compliance report required	• Avoid any statements on awarding of the contract until the process has been finalised • Avoid encouraging any bidder to incur costs (over and above the cost of tendering) before the contract is signed • Include in request documentation a statement that a contract will only be created on signature of a written agreement: seek legal advice
Unsuitable consultant selected	• Outputs below expectations • Output does not represent value for money	• Ask referees about any bad experiences with the consultant, as well as good ones • Include an informed 'outsider' on the evaluation committee to increase range of judgements • Re-tender if no bidder suitable, even if time is lost
Breach of due process or confidentiality during debriefing	• Loss of confidence by suppliers in agency processes • Ministerial representations • Possible legal action • Non-compliance report required	• During the debrief, compare tenderers' response only against evaluation criteria stated in request documentation, not against responses from other tenderers • Do not disclose any information provided by other tenderers • Involve other staff in the debriefing in case corroboration is needed • Place on file notes of debriefing session as soon as possible • Aim for professional, positive debriefing to foster goodwill

Type of risk	Likely consequence	Mitigation strategy
Apparent agreement masks different expectations between client and consultant	• Disputes during project	• Develop a clear specification of requirements • Include in request documentation the draft contract, a list of respective roles and responsibilities, etc. • Record all discussions during tendering and selection processes • Clarify all outstanding matters before signature of contract

6

Executing the contract

Some basics

The following points set out the basic principles and steps to follow when executing the contract:

- Where appropriate, involve legal and probity advisers at an early stage—ideally as far back as the preparation of a business case for the procurement.
- Exercise caution in discussions prior to signature to avoid 'drifting' into an implied or premature contract.
- Consider using trained negotiators in complex or high-value cases.
- Ensure that the entity's accountability to parliament for financial management and administration is not compromised, particularly through inappropriate use of confidentiality clauses.
- Clear up all outstanding issues before signing.
- Check that all Commonwealth Procurement Rules (CPRs) have been addressed.
- Before signature, check the final draft contract with a legal adviser.
- *Always* sign the contract before the commencement of the consultancy. Until signing has occurred, do not ask the consultant to undertake any work, even on an informal basis.
- Ensure that mandatory Australian Government reporting requirements are fulfilled on time.

Australian Government requirements

Accountability and transparency requirements

Requirements designed to promote the transparency of relevant entities' procurements are outlined in Chapter 7 of the CPRs. The key requirements include:

- Contracts and amendments must be reported on AusTender within 42 days by NCCEs for values above $10,000 and $400,000 for CCEs. All standing offers, regardless of value, must be reported on AusTender within 42 days. See clause 7.16 of the CPRs.

- The Senate of the Australian Parliament imposes an additional transparency requirement in the form of a Senate Order (the so-called Murray Motion). The order requires each NCCE to develop an internet listing twice a year that identifies contracts entered into during the preceding calendar or financial year, valued at or above $100,000 (GST inclusive), along with details relating to each of those contracts. The Department of Finance now publishes the reports on AusTender on behalf of NCCEs. However, ministers are still required to table in the Senate letters of advice that the NCCEs that they administer have placed a list on the internet (RMG no. 403 provides a letter template, as well as detailed administrative information regarding the Senate Order). Letters must be tabled within two months of the end of the reporting period to which they refer.

- A relevant entity's Annual Report must also include procurement information (CPR clause 7.24).

- Accountable authorities are required by sections 19 and 91 of the *Public Governance, Performance and Accountability Act 2013* (PGPA Act) (and clause 7.24 of the CPRs) to provide an annual report on compliance (and non-compliance) within the PGPA framework. The report must be provided to the Finance Minister as well as the entity's responsible minister. Detailed requirements are set out in Department of Finance (2015) RMG no. 208.

Tips and traps

Contract termination clauses are necessary, but may be of limited use in themselves. For example, one agency signed an IT management contract which contained a termination clause that could be activated under a large number of situations and conditions. (The contractor also supplied all of the entity's hardware as part of the contract.) However, termination of the contract would have left the agency with no IT support unless other contractors could be found to immediately take over a system with which they were not familiar, as well as providing all the equipment. An alternative approach would have been to also include **graduated incentives and penalties** that could be applied progressively if contract performance fell below expected standards.

Table 6. Executing the contract: Risks and mitigation

Type of risk	Likely consequence	Mitigation strategy
Deadlock on details of agreement	• Delays in delivery • Need to re-tender • Increased cost	• Include the draft contract in tender documentation • Distinguish between essential and non-essential requirements • Seek legal advice
Failure to ensure agency accountability to parliament	• Undue political and media attention • Accountable Authority must report non-compliance	• Familiarisation with CPRs and RMGs
Contract signed before all issues agreed	• Disputes during project • Project delay, or non-completion • Possible legal action	• Resolve all issues before signature, possibly through use of a trained mediator • If start time is critical, consult legal advisers about possible two-part contract • Consider long-term benefits of restarting the procurement process instead of continuing
Price and exchange rate fluctuations	• Cost over-runs	• Agree pricing schedules • Agree triggers for pricing variations • Hedge exchange rates, if relevant

Type of risk	Likely consequence	Mitigation strategy
Legal meaning of contract wording differs from intention	• Disputes • Project delay • Legal action	• Check final draft with legal advisers before signature • Ensure from outset the development of a collaborative relationship with the consultant, rather than an adversarial or overly legalistic approach • Include specific evaluation criteria for assessments during and at completion of contract

7

Contract and project management

Some basics

Consultants need to be managed, but not supervised or controlled.

No fail-safe methodology or perfect 'cookbook' approach exists for managing consultants, any more than it does for managing other human relationships. The key is to establish a sound, open working relationship. But a written contract that includes clauses on termination, arbitration, and graduated incentives and penalties can be a useful complement to the relationship.

If you have chosen competent consultants, let them get on with the job. That is why you have employed them, rather than using employees. But in managing them:

- Ensure not only that you have a clear understanding of what is needed, but that you communicate your requirements clearly.
- Appoint a project officer for all formal contact with the consultant to avoid involving 'too many cooks'.
- Ensure that payment schedules are aligned with the milestones specified in the contract.
- Steering committees can be very useful, particularly where there are many stakeholders in the project. But such committees also need to be managed firmly to avoid undue interference in the consultant's main task.

- Insist on regular (e.g. weekly) face-to-face meetings. Have the consultant produce an issues log at each meeting to ensure accountability. But remember, unnecessarily prolonged meetings cost money and send the wrong signal to the consultant about your own professionalism and desire to get the job done on time.

- Maintain 'open door' practices to ensure that communication is always possible.

In other words, treat a consultant as you would a member of staff who is a self-starter, professionally competent and highly motivated. Good consultants also seek regular feedback from clients to ensure that there are 'no surprises' at the end of the project. Their desire for repeat business from you makes them receptive to suggestions, but positively expressed feedback is always the most effective.

Subcontractors employed by consultants should be managed directly by them, not by you. The consultant should also be held fully responsible for the quality of their subcontractors' outputs. In the case of complex projects, it may be worth contracting another consultant separately to act as project manager. Where there is any variation in the scope of the work, it is in both parties' interests to exchange a written record of the change, as a formal contract variation.

Terminating a contract can turn the tables

The Amann Aviation case is an example where termination of a contract backfired.

In March 1987, Amann Aviation won the contract to provide coastal surveillance services in northern Australia. Although it did not at the time have the scale of operations or the expertise or equipment to meet the contract, it was to acquire resources before commencement of the contract in September. Its tender had indicated that acquisition of resources was feasible, but, in practice, it was apparent that the company was not in a position to begin operations by the start-up date. The Commonwealth therefore terminated the contract. In a subsequent court case, damages of over $5m were awarded against the Commonwealth. (Based on Senate Finance and Public Administration References Committee 1998: 13)

Using the Amann case as an example, Seddon (2004, 1.18) highlights the legal risks involved in terminating a contract. Wrongfully terminating a contract is itself a serious breach of a contract 'which then provides the other party with the right to terminate and seek damages'. Seddon points out that:

'In the Amann Aviation case the mistake made by the Commonwealth was to by-pass the show cause procedure that was written into the contract. The Commonwealth proceeded straight to termination without giving the contractor an opportunity to show cause [why the contract should not be terminated for breach of contract by Amann].' (Seddon 2004: 31, footnote 115)

Seddon (2004: 12) also draws attention to judicial authority supporting the principle that 'the government is required to adhere to higher standards of conduct than is expected of private sector entities [Government as a "moral exemplar"]'. The principle may be interpreted in particular cases as posing a dilemma for government (Seddon: 15) because it must act both in the interests of the beneficiary (the people it represents), as well as the contractor (a citizen, or a business that could be destroyed if the full force of a contractual remedy were exercised).

Australian Government requirements

There are no specific Australian Government requirements for managing consultants, but clause 6.6 of the CPRs does impose an obligation on officials to act ethically throughout a procurement. Officials should also check their entity's Accountable Authority Instructions and any other operational guidelines.

The Commonwealth Contract Terms (see RMG no. 420), include a provision C.C.1 that states that the parties agree to 'communicate openly with each other and co-operate in achieving the contractual objectives', to 'act honestly and ethically', as well as other collaborative commitments.

Tips and traps

* The consultant may not be fully informed about your agency or your area's role within it. It is worthwhile allocating some time to **educating the consultant** about your agency, including the structure, its major objectives, the political landscape, the culture, common abbreviations or acronyms used, and anything else that will assist in enhancing the quality and timeliness of output.

* For larger projects (or even small, complex ones), it is reasonable to expect the consultant to produce a **project charter** (plan) before starting work. Based on discussion with the client, it should include information like the terms of reference for the project, methodologies and a risk analysis for each component of the project, a budget that includes the payments schedule, a schedule of project meetings, timelines and milestones (often in the form of a Gantt chart), a protocol on any collaborative approaches, details

of specific client and consultant responsibilities, and any other relevant information about the project. The charter then becomes the basic reference document for both parties, and should form the basis for managing the project.

- Consultants will tend to feel aggrieved if they do additional work, but are then not paid for it. It is therefore important to ensure that a consultant does not undertake more work than is actually required without prior written agreement from the client. The contract itself should contain a clause that precludes the consultant from undertaking additional work without formal agreement (see, for example, Commonwealth Contract Terms clause C.C.2). Any changes to the contract should be agreed formally in the form of a **variation to the contract**. A trap for the unwary is an informal discussion or agreement between a client and a consultant which is not treated at the time as a formal variation because of the spirit of cooperation that may exist, or because it does not seem to be important enough. Nevertheless, it always pays to record any agreement that implies a change in scope in the work being undertaken, even if only apparently minor. Such notes (including emails) should be filed as part of the normal record-keeping process.

- Where a variation is made to the scope or terms and conditions of a consultancy, care should be taken to ensure that the **change is defensible** against a claim that it did not allow for an appropriate level of competition, or consider 'value for money'. Such a claim could be made if the change were to alter the nature or size of the original contract to a significant extent. An alternative supplier could argue that they would have been able to offer a more competitive bid had the original tender requirement included the variation. Where a change is significant, it may be judicious to let a separate contract for the work involved. If in doubt, seek legal advice.

- The term **'sign off'** to a consultant means acceptance by the client of an output, in satisfaction of the contract. Once a stage of the project has been 'signed off', the consultant is entitled to expect that no further work needs to be done on it unless a variation to the contract is agreed. If necessary, offer a conditional sign-off when you need to reserve your position for some reason.

- For large or complex projects, it is important to keep an **issues log** to record major issues that arise. The task of keeping a log can be allocated to the consultant by agreement, or, better still, specified as a requirement in request documentation. The log should form the basis of discussion during project meetings, and can be used for accountability purposes or to resolve disputes. Issues can be divided into 'open' (current) issues and 'closed' (resolved) issues. As open issues are resolved, they are moved (cut and pasted in electronic form) to the 'closed' table to maintain a historical record. The following is an example.

Exhibit 7.1. Sample issues log A: Open issues

No.	Date	Open issue	Resolution	Date
21	12 Jul	Budgetary implications of recommendations need to be assessed before Additional Estimates	13 Jul meeting: keep under review	
28	14 Jul	Consultant requested to attend special meeting with another agency	20 Aug: difficulties in arranging meeting due to inter-agency policy differences	
51	15 Oct	Consultant asked to confirm that project is on track, and that no extra work was being done that would lead to a claim for additional fees	15 Oct: on track 23 Dec: reconfirmed	

Exhibit 7.2. Sample issues log B: Closed issues

No.	Date	Closed issue	Resolution	Date
1	15 Jan	Consultant requires clarification of process for claiming expenses	15 Jan: agreed that tax invoices to be submitted to Mr Smith	15 Jan
2	23 Jan	Consultant raised problems regarding data base	23 Jan: agreed that Ms Jones will check data 25 Feb: IT section requested to provide software to enable transfer of revised data to consultant 26 Feb: consultant confirms receipt of data	26 Feb
3	12 Feb	etc.	etc.	

- Tender submissions and contracts normally specify the personnel to be engaged on a project. But consultants may leave a firm, or they may be engaged on another job by the time the project begins. Should you insist that only the originally **nominated personnel** be used? If you entered into the agreement because you knew the personnel nominated and wanted their particular skills, the answer is probably 'yes', if that is still feasible. Where this factor is important, seek a contractual guarantee (perhaps combined with monetary penalties for non-performance) at the time of selection of the consultant. Clause C.C.14 of the Commonwealth Contract Terms requires a supplier to seek the prior written consent of the client before replacing specified personnel.

- Project managers are pivotal to the success of any consultancy. They need to be across all of the key issues, understand the broader political context in which the client operates, possess business skills, and have good people skills. Some large firms have on occasion, however, used **inexperienced personnel** with little or no supervision in the role of project manager, presumably because of shortages of experienced staff. However, it is not the client's role to provide a training ground for project managers. If you are concerned about the skills possessed by the project manager, raise the issue as soon as possible with the firm's partner responsible for the job.

- Consultants measure jobs in terms of **'(consulting) days'**: the number of days (e.g. 7.5 hours per day) required to finish the work. Six days means six days of a consultant's overall time. It does not mean six days from the time of agreement to proceed with the work (elapsed time). Often there is considerable down-time during a job while a consultant waits for information to come in: for example, survey returns, or client-furnished data. Further, most consultants need to be engaged on several projects at the same time to earn sufficient income, unless the projects are large. Agencies that make best use of consultants are usually those that understand that consultants rarely work on a single issue. Consultants should certainly be expected to be responsive to your needs, but don't expect them to be dedicated solely to your project unless you have a prior agreement to this effect.

- A **steering committee** is sometimes used to oversee the work of the consultant. The establishment of a steering committee may be desirable where several stakeholders wish to be closely involved in the project, or the extent of the work warrants it. However, individual members of such committees can, on occasion, become caught up with unnecessary detail, or may insist on directing the consultant to pursue cherished but possibly irrelevant lines of inquiry that result in 'mission creep'. Consultants are often exasperated by steering committees whose members do not bother reading (let alone commenting on) drafts or documentation supplied during the project. At other times, steering committees may spend their time going through drafts page by page, more concerned with grammar and punctuation than with content. There appears to be no easy solution to such problems, but it helps if the Chair of the committee is experienced. The Chair should possesses sufficient authority to maintain members' focus on the main objectives of the consultancy, and should ensure that necessary decisions are taken, and approval ('sign-off') given, as stages of the project are completed successfully by the consultant. It also helps if the client's project officer and the consultant work together to caucus members of the steering committee out of session: committees often feel more comfortable taking decisions if their members are already 'familiar' with issues or solutions because they have already been explained to them beforehand. Meetings of the client, the project officer, the consultant and the Chair of the committee immediately before steering committee meetings can be very useful in discussing tactics and in briefing the Chair on the key issues.

- Insistence on adherence to public service **hierarchies** can be counterproductive. One consultant recalls working for a non-Commonwealth government agency whose CEO barred the project manager from attending meetings of the steering committee because he was too junior. Because only the senior manager was allowed to attend, it was difficult to keep in touch with a lot of the committee's thinking, or to develop a cooperative approach to the project.

- Prior agreement to **settle disputes** in a non-adversarial manner is an integral part of a collaborative arrangement. Where relationships have broken down badly, however, it may be worth considering mediation or even arbitration. Provision for such eventualities should be made in the contract.

- One public service official encountered a **recalcitrant consultant** who often promised delivery of a draft in the evening, but would normally deliver it only the next day. Faced with a time-critical deadline, the officer informed the consultant that he would wait in the office that night until the report was delivered. While the tactic was successful, it came at some personal cost to the officer concerned. An alternative approach might be to ensure that the contract contains sufficient flexibility in terms of imposing monetary penalties (or awarding benefits) in order to manage such situations.

- Despite popular belief in some quarters, consultants get little satisfaction from being **engaged unproductively**, whether they are paid or not. One consultant recalls being instructed by his partner to stop attending the many general, unfocused meetings called by the public service client. The partner agreed that the consultant was adding little value to the project by attending meetings of marginal relevance, despite recovering in fees the time spent doing so. Equally important in the decision was the fact that the consultant was working unreasonable hours because he was unable to meet deadlines for deliverables due to the time spent in meetings.

- An important benefit of using skilled consultants is that they can act as a sounding board, or provide new ideas. Despite some misconceptions among public servants, there is nothing wrong with **testing ideas**—even differing viewpoints within the agency— with a consultant. But it is important to first have consensus and clarity of purpose about the final output that is to be achieved by the consultant.

- In the absence of an obvious methodology, or where information is scarce, a first, 'knee-jerk' response in the public service is often to **conduct a survey**. But surveys are not always necessary, or even the best means of obtaining data. (Sometimes an enthusiastic consultant or client will wish to collect information out of interest, rather than out of necessity.) Before agreeing to incur the costs of a survey (including the time taken), insist on the consultant specifying exactly the issues or hypotheses which are to be tested, the specific statistical tests which will be used to determine confidence in the results, how each of the intended questions to be asked will be used to test a hypothesis, and why existing information cannot be used.

Even if a survey is found to be necessary, the process of justifying it will help to sharpen its focus, and avoid inclusion of unnecessary questions. Further, Australian government agencies proposing to conduct a survey of 50 or more businesses need to seek clearance through the Australian Bureau of Statistics' Statistical Clearing House: www.sch.abs.gov.au.

• For good reason, government agencies sometimes seek to achieve a transfer of knowledge from the consultant to themselves by including their own staff on the project team to work alongside the consultant. Unless such **nominated staff** are actually made available (and have the right skills), however, there is a high risk that the project will be delayed. Further, the consultant may have bid for the job on the basis that the client would contribute a certain amount of staff resources. If these resources are not made available, or are not suitable for the task, consultants may seek a variation to the contract to reflect the fact that they need to commit more of their own resources.

• At least one Commonwealth entity has encountered potential problems with consultants and contractors being employed over **extended periods of time**. In one case, all of the entity's employees working in the area had left over time, so the consultant effectively became the only repository of corporate knowledge. In other cases, consultants have been provided with necessary training (at taxpayer cost) as projects have progressed, in order to upgrade their skills to requisite standards. Such situations may reflect short-term needs or expediency, but they also raise questions about the employment of consultants rather than use of permanent staff. There is also the risk of the consultant effectively becoming a de facto employee, so that the entity becomes liable for superannuation contributions and other legislative provisions.

• Consultants' **invoices** are usually presented after delivery of 'milestone' outputs, or at the end of the month in the case of reimbursable expenses. Let the consultant know how you want invoices prepared: detailed accounts show more clearly what you are paying for. Good consultants will automatically provide a fair degree of information as a means of engendering trust. But unless you have a need for specific detail, don't ask for too much. The purpose is to satisfy accountability requirements. An invoice broken down into broad headings such as project meetings, report preparation, project management, air fares, taxi fares, etc., can usually provide sufficient information.

- For contracts valued up to $1 million, it is standard to provide for **payment** no later than 30 days after the date of receipt by an NCCE of a correctly rendered invoice. However, it is permitted to arrange for payment within a shorter period (Department of Finance 2014, RMG no. 417). If possible, arrange for your finance area to pay your consultant in less than 30 days. If you don't think that this will help create a better working relationship, ask yourself how you would feel if your salary was always paid 30 days in arrears.

- There is always the danger that a **risk management** plan, once produced, will be filed away and forgotten due to a misplaced feeling of having accomplished the 'task' merely by considering the issue. This danger can be ameliorated by ensuring that project management meetings include as a regular agenda item the review, and any updating, of the plan. The risk management plan itself should record the specific person responsible for implementing each of the mitigation strategies, what resources are to be utilised, the timetable for implementation, and the review mechanism. Incorporation of the risk management plan in the project charter (see above) is a useful way of keeping it in mind.

- Most public service guides to using consultants stress the need for **ethical behaviour**. Given the fairly general nature of this advice, it may not always be treated with the sense of immediacy that it deserves. A more pragmatic perspective is to ensure that all action taken during the course of a project is consistent with the *Public Service Act 1999*. Clause 6.6 of the CPRs further specifies the behaviour required of officials throughout a procurement.

Table 7. Contract and project management: Risks and mitigation

Type of risk	Likely consequence	Mitigation strategy
Consultant begins work before the contract is issued	• Claims for unauthorised work • Possible legal action by consultant for perceived breach of contract	• Avoid providing any encouragement to the consultant to start work before contract execution • Seek legal advice if problems are expected • Where time is short, consider a separate formal contract covering preliminary work
Unauthorised increase in scope of work	• Unanticipated increase in cost • Contract disputes • Possible legal action	• Maintain an issues log • Insist on regular, documented meetings and/or progress reports • Issue formal contract amendments for all agreed variations
Inadequate contract administration	• Cost increases • Failure of the project • Contract disputes • Possible legal action • Loss of intellectual property	• Maintain an issues log • Use trained staff • For large or complex projects, consider mediation, or use another consultant to manage the project • Track and report intellectual property issues
Failure to fulfil contract conditions, including delivery on time	• Contract disputes • Possible legal action • Client's needs not met	• Maintain an issues log • Foster collaborative and open working relationship • Insist on regular, documented meetings and/or progress reports • Issue formal contract amendments for all agreed variations to work • Maintain strict control over payments according to observable milestones • Where quantifiable loss occurs, consider seeking liquidated damages
Client fails to take decisions, or to provide nominated staff	• Project delay • Possible budget over-run • Possible variation to contract, or legal action	• Ensure that decisions are taken quickly, including 'sign-off' on satisfactory delivery of outputs • Appoint Chair of steering committee who has authority and experience • Ensure that staff nominated to work alongside the consultant are available and possess relevant skills

8

Closure

Some basics

It is likely that payments will have been made against observable milestones during the course of the project. Finalisation of the project will thus generally involve only the completion of the final milestone(s).

Once a client has 'signed off' on a project (or milestone), the consultant is entitled to consider the job (or part thereof) to be complete. It is therefore important that final acceptance ('signing off') does not occur without prior reconciliation of all outputs against those specified in the contract. The reconciliation should obviously take place early enough for remedial action or additional work to be undertaken if necessary.

The main factors to check during a reconciliation include:

- Have all deliverables specified in the contract been provided?
- Is the quality of the deliverables satisfactory?
- Is there a need to take into account any new circumstances to ensure that the deliverables are current and relevant?
- Were all outputs delivered on time, or as part of an agreed variation?
- Have all expenses incurred by the consultant been authorised and approved for payment?
- Overall, have the objectives of the project been met by the deliverables?

Where a collaborative relationship has been maintained with the consultant, and variations to the contract have been documented throughout, there should be little difficulty in agreeing on the final deliverables. If an issues log has been used throughout the procurement, reconciliation should not be a major chore.

Should difficulties nevertheless arise, consult your agency's legal adviser immediately.

Australian Government requirements

Considerable time can elapse between completion of a consultancy and subsequent requests for information arising from an audit of the procurement process, Freedom of Information requests, legal proceedings, etc. Because memories fade and personnel move on, corporate knowledge can be lost unless records are brought fully up-to-date while details are still fresh in one's mind. If needed later, the information can be found more easily on the relevant file.

Clause 7.2 of the CPRs also requires that documentation relating to a procurement be retained in accordance with the *Archives Act 1983*.

Risk management

The main risk at the end of a project is that a final output will be delivered by the consultant, and payment made, without a proper check that the deliverables specified in the contract have all been provided. An obvious mitigation strategy is therefore to conduct a thorough reconciliation of output received from the consultant against the outputs specified in the contract.

The reconciliation should take place with sufficient time to spare for additional work by the consultant, if required. Also, don't forget to include any contract variations in the reconciliation process.

Tips and traps

- One agency let a consultancy with very short timeframes. Material was to be prepared in stages for a manual, prior to printing and presentation at a training course. Asked by the consultant to **'sign off'** on the chapters of the manual as they were completed, the agency's contact officer did so, but subsequently requested substantial revisions after the manual had been sent to the printer. Because of the short timeframes involved, course participants did not gain access to the manual. The entity's own required training outcome was thus compromised, and the consultant was made to look less than competent. Apart from the contract management aspects of this case, it is important to recognise that 'sign off' to a consultant really means final acceptance of the product in satisfaction of the contract.

- Sometimes, consultants request a **'sign-off' meeting**. Their expectation is that, unless any major issues are raised, the meeting itself constitutes sign-off by the client. Make it clear that you reserve your position until all documentation, including any reports, have been properly considered and finalised.

9

Review

Some basics

Even if a project has been completed successfully, it is still possible to gain some additional useful knowledge. Good consultants will be prepared to assist in this process, and some also provide evaluation forms to clients (or conduct interviews) in order to gain feedback for their own staff.

Busy managers are unlikely to be able to afford the time to engage in an extensive review process. However, even a *brief* review can:

- provide an opportunity to discuss with the consultant his or her view on how the results can best be used—an external perspective from someone who, by the end of the project, has a good grasp of the subject matter, can be invaluable;
- provide a learning experience for all staff;
- improve your own contract management skills; and,
- identify further value to be gained (for example, in making available to the public or the minister for media purposes any useful data collected).

The review should focus on major issues, not the nitty-gritty:

- Could project objectives have been better defined?
- Was there enough (or too much) management of the consultant?
- How could the consultant have performed better?

- Have enough skills been transferred to your staff?
- Which risks were not identified properly before the project started?
- How useful are the results compared to the original objectives?
- How could the client have performed better?

Australian Government requirements

There are no specific guidelines or requirements for reviewing a consultancy. Nevertheless, accountability and good practice also imply that an evaluation should be carried out and documented as a matter of course.

Officials are required by CPR clause 7.2 to maintain 'a level of documentation commensurate with the scale, scope and risk of the procurement', and CPR clause 7.24 requires disclosure of non-compliance with the CPRs. CPR clause 4.14 further provides that 'when a contract does not specify an end date it must allow for periodic review and subsequent termination of the contract by the relevant entity, if the relevant entity determines that it does not continue to represent value for money'.

Tips and traps

- A review should cover more than just the management and output from the consultancy itself. To be useful, it should also include the process of initiating the consultancy (including the justification) and the subsequent use of outputs for policy formulation, organisational change, or other purpose. In essence, the review should **test whether the initial objectives have been satisfied** and identify lessons learned. It should not be used as an excuse to lay blame for problems encountered on the way.
- Additional value can be extracted from a consultancy if the consultant provides a general debriefing on the project. Consultants often pick up **additional information** that is of use to the client but is not included in a report because it is not directly relevant in purely contractual terms. Similarly, consultants can brief clients on

any avenues investigated that were 'dead ends': such information may not appear in a report, but helps provide a more complete picture of the issues investigated.

- Where consultants are hired regularly, a file containing **'lessons learned'** is often useful, particularly if it includes basic details such as the nature of the project and the entity involved. New staff, or those with less experience in letting contracts can skim the file to gain an impression of pitfalls to avoid, and useful practices to emulate.

- To a certain extent, successful use of consultants requires practical experience. It is therefore a good idea to invite **all of your staff**, not just those who were involved directly, to sit in on reviews. The knowledge gained will be at least as valuable as anything that can be gleaned from publications, and will contribute to improve use of consultants in the future.

- Reviews can also be carried out **before the finalisation of a project**. In large projects, it may even pay to seek external review of request documentation before its release, particularly where subject matter expertise is important.

- It may not be realistic to expect busy public service managers to carry out a review of every project. However, Commonwealth entities seeking to improve their general level of performance in letting consultancies could select a number of projects each year for use as **case studies** in a 'no-blame' atmosphere to allow all staff to learn from them. It would be important, however, to ensure that the entity's own performance (for example, turnaround time for selecting a consultant) were assessed, as well as the performance of the consultant. An alternative is to link performance assessment directly to the outcomes of a consultancy project.

- Where **useful data or information** has been collected and there is a likelihood that it may be of use to researchers or policymakers elsewhere, it is worth weighing the costs and benefits of making it accessible. Dissemination to academics and state or local governments, reference to its availability in your entity's annual report, or posting on a website, can help make it more generally available. From a national perspective, resources will be saved in future if data or information collection does not need to be duplicated.

Table 8. Evaluation: Risks and mitigation

Type of risk	Likely consequence	Mitigation strategy
Consultant resents contract review	• Inadequate evaluation • Damage to relationship between client and consultant	• Foster collaborative relationship with consultant throughout project • Hold regular reviews as part of contract management process, rather than one at the end • Make clear from outset (including in request documentation) that final review is to occur • Include review clause in contract
Failure to identify problems and address them	• Missed opportunity to improve future procurement activity	• Develop systematic evaluation methods and techniques • Use clear, relevant evaluation criteria

10

What if things go wrong?

Some basics

Every project is different. There is no way of predicting the range of things that can go wrong. And things can go wrong at any stage of a project.

Risk can be minimised by implementing risk mitigation measures such as those outlined in each of the chapters above.

However, it is important to realise that some of the protective measures that are available can, and should, be used:

- Graduated rewards and penalties can be used to advantage where there are early indications of problems developing.
- In some cases, it may be worth approaching a consultant's superiors if performance is below standard.
- In extreme cases, a project can be terminated. Despite the cost, it may be better to simply start again. But seek legal advice first.

Things can go wrong at any stage of a project. Any of the following may (or may not) presage a problem:

- An **exclusive approach** by the consultant, often characterised by the 'just leave it all to us, we'll fix it' attitude. It is often accompanied by an attitude that public servants don't really know what they are doing. One symptom noted by an entity that experienced this attitude was persistent late arrival for meetings, a problem that was remedied by protesting to the firm's hierarchy.

- The corollary is a dismissive attitude by government entities whose staff treat **consultants with contempt**. Treat consultants as you would your own staff. Good people management practice ultimately generates better results.

- A **breakdown in communication**. Good consultants make a point of regularly (at least once a week, but on a daily basis for some projects) checking with the client that everything is proceeding satisfactorily. Not touching base may be a sign that things are not going too well. Take the initiative to re-establish contact yourself, and find out how things are going.

- The corollary from the consultant's perspective is when the client begins to **'walk away'** from the job. When clients plead too much work to be able to take a direct interest, or suggest that the consultant 'just get on with it yourself', or find some other means of distancing themselves from the project, consultants begin to worry about being able to achieve a successful outcome.

- Excessive **'library research'**. Too much general research may indicate that the consultant does not have sufficient expertise in the area.

- Excessive focus on **producing a report**, rather than dealing with issues or people. This is particularly relevant in choosing consultants to implement programs that involve organisational change. Unless there is a shortage of reports on your bookshelf, look for a consultant who is geared to solving problems rather than just documenting them.

- Use of **'guru language'**. If a consultant suggests 'leveraging off the knowledge base to achieve optimal organisational alignment in a contextual framework going forward', find one who uses plain English.

- Undue focus on the use of software or an analytical package as the primary means of analysing issues or solving problems. An analytical framework is essential in problem-solving, but beware the **'package bender'** who only knows one technique and tries to adapt it to every situation. A good check during the selection process is to ask what alternative approaches could be used.

- A too-ready willingness to drop the **bid price** during negotiations may indicate that a consultant has difficulty in finding other work at the bid price. Good, sought-after consulting firms will often refuse to materially alter their bid price without also redefining the scope of the project.

- **Staff nominated by the client** to work alongside the consultant find it difficult to contribute, because of insufficient skills or because of other work priorities. Unless alternative resources are made available to the consultant, delay (or higher cost) is likely.

- The client, or a steering committee, focuses on **red herrings**, avoids or postpones taking decisions, or **vacillates** in providing 'sign-off' as the stages of a project are completed.

- **Persistent delays** or regular attempts to redefine the scope of the work. On the other hand, occasional delays, or necessary redefinition of issues may be an indication of a high-quality consultant.

- Once a client or a consultant has started to **refer to the provisions of the contract**, the relationship is probably in serious trouble.

Prevention of problems is invariably preferable to any cures. So it is important to be aware of major warning signals. Because this publication is written from an Australian Public Service perspective, most of the issues raised here could be misinterpreted as implying that the consultant is invariably responsible for any problems. However, consultants may also come to feel aggrieved during the course of a contract. As the use of consultants increases, and the CPRs become more directive, the likelihood of legal action against the Australian Government is also likely to rise.

Seeking some degree of legal advice at all stages of a procurement is a worthwhile risk-reduction strategy. Advice should definitely be sought quickly if things do start to go wrong. Management decisions on what to do next are always better if they are fully informed about the options available.

Appendix A: Glossary

Where available, the terms in this glossary have been reproduced from the Commonwealth Procurement Rules, associated legislation, and other documents published by the Australian Government Department of Finance.

Accountable Authority: section 12 of the PGPA Act specifies the accountable authority of a 'Commonwealth entity'. In the case of a Department of State, it is the Secretary of the Department. Prior to 1 July 2014, known as 'Chief Executive' under the FMA Act, and as 'Director, or Governing Board' under the CAC Act.

Accountable Authority Instructions (AAIs): accountable authorities can issue instructions as a mechanism to provide their officials with guidance regarding the key principles and requirements of the resource management framework, including for procurement activity. Under the FMA Act, known as the Chief Executive Instructions. See also Department of Finance (2015) RMG no. 206, www.finance.gov.au/resource-management/index.

Annual Procurement Plan: clauses 7.7 and 7.8 of the CPRs state that 'each relevant entity must maintain on AusTender a current procurement plan containing a short strategic procurement outlook. The annual procurement plan should include the subject matter of any significant planned procurement and the estimated publication date of the approach to market. Relevant entities should update their plans regularly throughout the year'.

Approach to market (ATM): any notice inviting potential suppliers to participate in a procurement which may include a request for tender, request for quote, request for expression of interest, request for application for inclusion on a multi-use list, request for information or request for proposal. The abbreviation 'ATM' is used on AusTender and other procurement documents to reference an approach to market.

Arrangement: a contract, agreement, deed or understanding (section 23, PGPA Act).

AusTender: AusTender is the system used to enable relevant entities to meet their publishing obligations under the CPRs. It also enables relevant entities to monitor and review their AusTender-based procurements, including approaches to market, publication of contracts and multi-use lists, and amendments to contracts and multi-use lists. It is available at www.tenders.gov.au. See also CPR clauses 7.5 to 7.13.

CAC Act: *Commonwealth Authorities and Companies Act 1997.* The Act was replaced by the *Public Governance, Performance and Accountability Act 2013* (PGPA Act) from 1 July 2014.

Commonwealth Contracting Suite (CCS): a template set of contracting documents that must generally be used by Non-Corporate Commonwealth Entities for procurements below $200,000 (including GST). See Department of Finance (2015) RMG no. 420: www.finance. gov.au/resource-management/index.

Commonwealth entity: Chapter 2 of the PGPA Act defines various forms of Commonwealth entities, including a Department of State, a Parliamentary Department, a body corporate established under Commonwealth legislation, etc. See 'Non-Corporate Commonwealth Entity' and 'Corporate Commonwealth Entity'.

Commonwealth Procurement Rules (CPRs): The CPRs incorporate international obligations, government policy and good practice in procurement into a set of rules that apply to procurement by Australian Government entities. They are issued by the Minister for Finance under section 105B of the PGPA Act: www.finance.gov.au/ sites/default/files/2014%20Commonwealth%20Procurement%20 Rules.pdf. Achieving value for money is the core principle of the CPRs, which cover the whole process of procuring goods and services. From 1 July 2014, the CPRs replaced the Commonwealth Procurement Guidelines that had been established in 2005 under the FMA and CAC Acts.

Contract: an arrangement, as defined by s.23(2) of the PGPA Act, for the procurement of goods and services under which relevant money is payable or may become payable. Note: this includes standing offers and panels.

Corporate Commonwealth Entity (CCE): as defined in section 8 of the *Public Governance, Performance and Accountability Act 2013* (PGPA Act). Prior to 1 July 2014, known as a 'Commonwealth authority' under the CAC Act.

Deliverable: specific output, usually (and preferably) defined in the contract, or in a schedule to the contract.

Evaluation criteria: the criteria that are used to evaluate the compliance and/or relative ranking of submissions. Evaluation criteria must be clearly stated in the request documentation.

Expression of Interest: a response to an open approach to the market that requests submissions from businesses interested in participating in a procurement. The list of potential suppliers who have submitted expressions of interest may be used as the basis for conducting a select tender process.

FMA Act: *Financial Management and Accountability Act 1997*. The Act was supplemented by FMA Regulations (FMAR). The FMA Act was replaced by the *Public Governance, Performance and Accountability Act 2013* (PGPA Act) from 1 July 2014.

Issues log: a record of issues that arise during a project (see Chapter 7).

Limited tender: involves a relevant entity approaching one or more potential suppliers to make submissions, when the process does not meet the rules for open tender or pre-qualified tender. Limited tenders are subject to additional rules under Division 2 of the CPRs.

Liquidated damages: an agreed pre-estimate of damages for a specific breach of contract, such as late performance.

Listed entity: defined in section 8 (The Dictionary) of the PGPA Act to cover non-corporate bodies, persons, groups of persons or organisations, etc. Prior to 1 July 2014, known as a 'prescribed agency' under the FMA Act and FMA Regulations.

Memorandum of Understanding (MOU): formal agreement between two or more Non-Corporate Commonwealth Entities. An enforceable contract is not possible because the entities are both part of the same legal entity (the Australian Government), and the government cannot contract with itself.

Milestone: reference point specified in contract. Where a milestone represents a point of payment, it is important to ensure that the point is specified in terms of a clearly identifiable and measurable output by the consultant. Some contracts specify milestones as points of formal review of progress on which an extension or continuation of the contract might be based.

Minimum content and format requirements: criteria that a tenderer's submission is required to meet when responding to an approach to market in order to be eligible for further consideration in a procurement process.

Multi-use list: a list, intended for use in more than one procurement process, of pre-registered suppliers who have satisfied the conditions for participation on the list. Each approach to a multi-use list is considered to be a new procurement, but the process establishing a multi-use list is not in itself a procurement.

Murray Motion: On 20 June 2001, the Senate agreed to an order requiring ministers to table a letter, stating that PGPA Act entities falling under their responsibility have placed on the internet a list of contracts of $100,000 (GST inclusive) or more which are current or entered into during the previous 12 months. The Senate Order letters must be tabled within two months of the end of the reporting period to which the listing(s) relate. From 1 July 2015, reports are generated by the Department of Finance and published on the AusTender website on behalf of entities and can be accessed by the Senate Order button.

Nominated personnel: usually those identified in a contract as carrying out the actual work during the project, or as contact officers.

Non-corporate Commonwealth Entity (NCCE): defined in section 8 of the *Public Governance, Performance and Accountability Act 2013* (PGPA Act). Prior to 1 July 2014, known as an agency or FMA agency under the FMA Act.

Official: defined in section 8 of the *Public Governance, Performance and Accountability Act 2013* (PGPA Act). Prior to 1 July 2014, known as 'officer, staff or employee' under the FMA Act and FMA Regulations, and as 'officer, senior manager' under the CAC Act.

Open approach to market: any notice inviting all potential suppliers to participate in a procurement which may include a request for tender, request for quote, request for expression of interest, request for application for inclusion on a multi-use list, request for information and request for proposal.

Open book approach: in a collaborative arrangement, the risk of disagreement over fees and expenses can be reduced if the consultant permits the client full and open access to information on the consultant's costs throughout the project.

Open tender: involves publishing an open approach to market and inviting submissions.

Option: a legal right within a contract or deed of standing offer (panel) arrangement to unilaterally extend the term of the contract or panel by a specified period. An option must be exercised in accordance with the terms of the contract or deed of standing offer (for example, by notifying the other party of the intention to exercise the option). The exercise of an option is not a variation or an agreement to extend the contract or deed of standing offer. Exercising an option in a contract is not a procurement in itself. However, value for money considerations still apply. Entities should consider all relevant alternatives including approaching the market (see also 'Variation').

Panel: panel arrangements or contracts involve an agency pre-selecting a number of consultants. The selected consultants can be drawn on at any time to provide services at a price agreed when bidding for a place on the panel, without the need to go again to tender. Both the agency and the panel consultants gain from this arrangement because there is no need to go through a tender process each time that work is required. Because of the cost savings to them, consultants may quote a lower fee when bidding to be part of a panel arrangement.

Partnering: a cooperative approach to the employment of consultants. It may involve the use of a 'relationship agreement'.

Period contract: an agreement to provide goods or services on particular terms over a period of time. A panel period contract means that standing offer arrangements have been entered into with more than one contractor or consultant for the provision of goods and services of the same type and nature.

Potential supplier: an entity or person who may respond to an approach to market.

Pre-qualified tender: involves publishing an approach to market inviting submissions from all potential suppliers on:

a.   a shortlist of potential suppliers that responded to an initial open approach to market on AusTender;

b.   a list of potential suppliers selected from a multi-use list established through an open approach to market; or

c.   a list of all potential suppliers that have been granted a specific licence or comply with a legal requirement, when the licence or compliance with the legal requirement is essential to the conduct of the procurement.

Process contract: a statement in the nature of a Request for Tender may itself constitute an offer which, upon acceptance, becomes a binding and enforceable contract, a so-called process contract. In other words, an agency that issues request documentation may be bound to follow the procedures and selection criteria specified in it. The courts may consider that the process contract contains an implied term that the agency will conduct its evaluation fairly and in a manner that ensures equal opportunity for all bidders.

Procurement: clauses 2.7 and 2.8 of the CPRs state that 'procurement encompasses the whole process of procuring goods and services. It begins when a need has been identified and a decision has been made on the procurement requirement. Procurement continues through the processes of risk assessment, seeking and evaluating alternative solutions, the awarding of a contract, the delivery of and payment for the goods and services and, where relevant, the ongoing management of the contract and consideration of disposal of goods. In addition to the acquisition of goods and services by a relevant entity for its own use, procurement includes the acquisition of goods and services on behalf of another relevant entity or a third party.'

Procurement threshold: the monetary procurement thresholds specified in clause 9.7 of the Commonwealth Procurement Rules require observance of the additional procurement rules contained in Division 2 of the CPRs. The thresholds are as follows:

a. for Non-Corporate Commonwealth Entities, other than for procurements of construction services, the procurement threshold is $80,000;

b. for prescribed Corporate Commonwealth Entities, other than for procurements of construction services, the procurement threshold is $400,000; or

c. for procurements of construction services by relevant entities, the procurement threshold is $7.5 million.

Project charter: essentially, a plan for managing the project. It should include information like the terms of reference for the project, methodologies and a risk analysis for each component of the project, a budget, a schedule of project meetings, milestones and payments against them, a protocol on collaborative behaviour, details of specific client and consultant responsibilities, and any other relevant information about the project. The charter then becomes the basic reference document for both parties, and should form the basis for managing the contract.

Project management plan: see project charter.

***Public Governance, Performance and Accountability Act 2013* (PGPA Act):** the key legislation that covers Australian Government resource management requirements. It provides a coherent framework encompassing the use of appropriations, commitment of money, banking arrangements, and the imposition of requirements regarding standards of governance, performance and accountability for 'Commonwealth entities'. The Act is administered by the Finance Minister, who may make rules and other legislative instruments under the Act. These instruments can be disallowed by parliament. The PGPA Act replaced the *Financial Management and Accountability Act 1997* and the *Commonwealth Authorities and Companies Act 1997*, which were repealed on 30 June 2014. An independent review of the PGPA Act will be conducted after July 2017 in accordance with section 112, and the Finance Minister will table the review in parliament.

Public Governance, Performance and Accountability Rule 2014 **(PGPAR):** the PGPAR is made under the PGPA Act. Prior to 1 July 2014, its equivalent was known as the 'FMA Regulations' which were formed under the FMA Act.

Relevant entity: the Commonwealth Procurement Rules (clause 2.2) refer to Non-Corporate Commonwealth Entities plus Corporate Commonwealth Entities listed in section 30 of the *Public Governance, Performance and Accountability Rule 2014* collectively as 'relevant entities'.

Relevant money: is money that a Commonwealth entity holds as cash or in bank accounts. It becomes committed when an entity undertakes an activity that results in an obligation to pay relevant money (RMG no. 400). Known as 'public money' prior to 1 July 2014 under the FMA Act, and as 'money held in own account' under the CAC Act.

Reporting requirements for procurements are outlined in Chapter 7 of the CPRs.

Request documentation: documentation provided to potential suppliers to enable them to understand and assess the requirements of the procuring relevant entity and to prepare appropriate and responsive submissions. This general term includes documentation for expressions of interest, multi-use lists, open tender, pre-qualified tender and limited tender.

Request for Expression of Interest (REI): see Expression of Interest.

Request for Proposal (RFP): usually sought following evaluation of responses to an REI, as a means of identifying innovative solutions. Parties are asked to provide a preliminary or a full tender proposal.

Request for Tender (RFT): a formal request that may be publicly advertised to obtain offers from potential suppliers of goods and services. An RFT normally contains a Statement of Requirement.

Sign-off: a client's acceptance of an intermediate or final output. Further work requested after formal 'sign-off' should be the subject of a variation or extension to the contract.

Small and Medium Enterprises (SMEs): an Australian or New Zealand firm with fewer than 200 full-time equivalent employees.

Specification: a description of the features of the goods and services to be procured.

Standing offer: an arrangement setting out the terms and conditions, including a basis for pricing, under which a supplier agrees to supply specified goods and services to a relevant entity for a specified period. It is sometimes called a panel where more than one supplier is involved. Because a procurement process has already been conducted to establish a standing offer (or panel), specific procurements can then be undertaken with any supplier on the panel.

Statement of Requirement (SOR): description of an activity or client needs in terms of outputs and constraints such as timeframes (see RFT).

Submission: any formally submitted response from a potential supplier to an approach to market. Submissions may include tenders, responses to expressions of interest, applications for inclusion on a multi-use list or responses to a request for quote.

Supplier: an entity or person who has entered into a contract with the Commonwealth.

Tender specification: document that provides information on the outputs and outcomes required from a consultant, including relevant quality standards.

Tenderer: an entity or person who has responded with a submission to an approach to market.

Threshold: see 'Procurement Threshold' above.

Value for Money: the core principle underpinning Australian Government procurement (see Chapter 4 of the Commonwealth Procurement Rules).

Variation: A variation to extend a contract or deed of standing offer beyond the terms of the original contract (rather than exercising an extension option within the terms of a contract), constitutes a new procurement that must be conducted in accordance with the CPRs. Variations to include new extension options generally increase the scope of the contract or panel arrangement and are therefore not allowed. Changes in terms and conditions should be recorded formally in a variation to the contract, in order to avoid later disputes and to ensure accountability (see also 'Option').

Appendix B: References and further reading

Australian Capital Territory Government procurement policy: www. business.act.gov.au/business_advice/grow_your_business/ government_procurement_and_tenders (accessed 10 January 2016).

Australian Government Solicitor (AGS) (1997a). 'Major changes in tendering law: the Hughes case', Legal Briefing no. 33, July, Canberra. Available from: www.ags.gov.au/publications/legal-briefing/br33.htm.

Australian Government Solicitor (AGS) (1997b). 'Competitive tendering and contracting', Legal Briefing no. 35, August, Canberra. Available from: www.ags.gov.au/publications/legal-briefing/br35.htm.

Australian Government Solicitor (AGS) (2014). 'Commonwealth Procurement Rules', Fact Sheet no. 7, December, Canberra. Available from: www.ags.gov.au/publications/fact-sheets/Fact_sheet_ No_7.pdf.

Australian Government Solicitor (AGS) (2015). 'Confidentiality considerations for tenders, funding programs and other government initiatives', Fact Sheet no. 25, February. Available from: www.ags. gov.au/publications/fact-sheets/Fact_sheet_No_25.pdf.

Australian National Audit Office (ANAO) (1997). *The Gun Buy-Back Scheme*, Audit Report no. 25, December, Canberra.

Australian National Audit Office (ANAO) (1998). *Selecting Suppliers: Managing the Risk*, Commonwealth of Australia, Canberra.

Australian National Audit Office (ANAO) (2003). *The Senate Order for Departmental and Agency Contracts* (Spring 2002 Compliance), Audit Report no. 32, Commonwealth of Australia, Canberra.

Department of Administrative Services (DAS) (1990). 'Contracting for consultancy services', Commonwealth Procurement Guideline no. 13, November, Canberra. (This publication is obsolete but contains some useful points.)

Department of Administrative Services (DAS) (1992). 'Managing risk in procurement', Commonwealth Procurement Guideline no. 8, June, Canberra. (This publication is obsolete but contains some useful points.)

Department of Finance (2014). Commonwealth Procurement Rules, Commonwealth of Australia, Canberra.

Department of Finance (2014). Commonwealth Risk Management Policy, www.finance.gov.au/comcover/risk-management/the-commonwealth-risk-management-policy.

Department of Finance (2014). Resource Management Guide no. 207: Government Policy Orders, Commonwealth of Australia, Canberra.

Department of Finance (2014). Resource Management Guide no. 400: Approving commitments of relevant money, Commonwealth of Australia, Canberra.

Department of Finance (2014). Resource Management Guide no. 411: Grants, procurements and other financial arrangements, Commonwealth of Australia, Canberra.

Department of Finance (2014). Resource Management Guide no. 417: Supplier pay on-time or pay interest policy, Commonwealth of Australia, Canberra.

Department of Finance (2015). Resource Management Guide no. 001: Commonwealth Resource Management Companion, Commonwealth of Australia, Canberra.

Department of Finance (2015). Resource Management Guide no. 206: Accountable Authority Instructions, Commonwealth of Australia, Canberra.

Department of Finance (2015) (archived). Resource Management Guide no. 208: PGPA Framework Compliance Reporting (archived as at 5 January 2016), Commonwealth of Australia, Canberra.

Department of Finance (2015). Resource Management Guide no. 403: Meeting the Senate Order on entity contracts, Commonwealth of Australia, Canberra.

Department of Finance (2015). Resource Management Guide no. 415: Commonwealth grants and procurement connected policies, Commonwealth of Australia, Canberra.

Department of Finance (2015). Resource Management Guide no. 420: Mandatory use of the Commonwealth Contracting Suite for procurement under $200,000, Commonwealth of Australia, Canberra.

Department of Finance and Administration and The Treasury (2004). *Australian Government Competitive Neutrality Guidelines for Managers*, Financial Management Guidance no. 9, February, Canberra.

New South Wales Government procurement policy: www.procurepoint.nsw.gov.au (accessed 10 January 2016).

Northern Territory Government procurement policy: www.dob.nt.gov.au/business/tenders-contracts/procurement-support/Pages/procurement-policy.aspx (accessed 10 January 2016).

Pearce, D (1993). *Independent Inquiry into the Circumstances Surrounding the Non-requirement of a Deposit for Satellite Pay-TV Licences, and Related Matters*, Report by Professor Dennis Pearce to the Secretary of the Department of Transport and Communications, 19 May 1993, Australian Government Publishing Service, Canberra.

Popovich, IS (1994). *Managing Consultants: The Manager's Book of Business Secrets*, Career Professionals, Newman, Western Australia.

Purchasing Australia (Department of Administrative Services) (1996). *Managing risk in procurement—a handbook*, Australian Government Publishing Service, Canberra.

Purchasing Australia (Department of Administrative Services) (1997). *Applying Risk Management Techniques to Complex Procurement*, Australian Government Publishing Service, Canberra.

Queensland Government procurement policy: www.qld.gov.au/gov/procurement-policy (accessed 10 January 2016).

Ross, C (2004). 'Managing Process Contracts', OnSite, Minter Ellison, August.

Seddon, N (2004). *Government Contracts: Federal, State and Local*, third edition, The Federation Press, NSW.

Shenson, HL (1990). *How to Select and Manage Consultants: A Guide to Getting What You Pay For*, Lexington Books, Massachusetts, USA.

South Australian Government procurement policy: www.spb.sa.gov.au/content/policies-guides (accessed 10 January 2016).

Tasmanian Government procurement policy: www.purchasing.tas.gov.au/buyingforgovernment (accessed 10 January 2016).

Victorian Government procurement policy: www.procurement.vic.gov.au/Home (accessed 10 January 2016).

Western Australian Government procurement policy: www.finance.wa.gov.au/cms/Government_Procurement.aspx (accessed 10 January 2016).

Yates, A (2000). *Government as an Informed Buyer: Recognising technical expertise as a crucial factor in the success of engineering contracts*, The Institution of Engineers, Australia, Canberra.

www.ingramcontent.com/pod-product-compliance
Lightning Source LLC
Chambersburg PA
CBHW051436270326
41935CB00019B/1839